Amber Earns Her Ears

My Secret Walt Disney World Cast Member Diary

Amber Michelle Sewell

Foreword by Lee Cockerell
Retired Executive Vice-President
Disney World Resort

Theme Park Press

Amber Earns Her Ears

First Printing 2013
ISBN 978-0-9843415-3-5

Editor: Bob McLain
Cover Design: Camille Rejenne Pavon
Layout: Artisanal Text
Publisher: Theme Park Press

Address queries and permission requests to:
bob@themeparkpress.com

If you have a Disney story to tell, Theme Park Press would like to help you tell it. We offer generous compensation and the most author-friendly terms in the business. See how we can put you in print:
www.ThemeParkPress.com/writeforus

Contents

Foreword

I PARTICULARLY ENJOYED READING *Amber Earns Her Ears*, as the Disney College Program touched me personally even before I joined Disney in 1990 to open the Euro Disney project in Paris.

Back in 1989, I was the General Manager of a Marriott Hotel, and my son Daniel was in his second year at Boston University. He called me asking for ideas on what summer job he should pursue to gain some experience in and exposure to a different industry. He had already worked at the Boston Copley Marriott as a waiter in the sports bar, and had done an internship at a Boston brokerage firm.

I suggested he try to get a job at Disney through the Disney College Program. I had heard lots of good things about this program and had, in fact, instructed my management team at Marriott to hire any applicant who had Disney experience. I was never disappointed in hiring someone who was Disney trained.

My son Daniel called me two weeks after he started the College Program and said, "Dad I have bad news for you. Disney is better than Marriott." I said, "Why are they better?" He replied, "The training is fabulous." A year later I was recruited by Disney. I tell people that my son got me the job.

Amber Sewell has done a great job of painting a fun and informative picture of what it is like to work and live at Disney as a young college student.

Her descriptions of her many experiences and escapades brought back fond and not-so-fond memories of similar stories I had heard from my son and from many of the thousands of young people who have participated in this program.

I suggest anyone looking for a once-in-a-lifetime experience consider the Disney College Program. I assure you that, like Amber, you will never be the same. Learning from the best will help you be the best, and will give you a lifelong edge. As one college professor told me a few years ago, "Lee, we sent you an introvert and you sent us back an extrovert."

The real value of doing the Disney College Program is that when you apply for a job after graduation, or even years later, the employer interviewing you will only want to talk about your Disney experience and how you can help their organization achieve service excellence like Disney does.

If you can't participate in the Disney College Program, I suggest you read *Amber Earns Her Ears* to gain a unique understanding of how the right experience can bring you lots of fun, frustration, and knowledge which will serve you well as you navigate your career. It sure worked out for my son, who is now the Vice President of Disney's Hollywood Studios. He has been with Disney for 20 years, and it all began when he earned his ears.

Lee Cockerell
Executive Vice President (Retired and Inspired)
Walt Disney World Resort
April 2013

Author of:
*Creating Magic: 10 Common Sense Leadership
Strategies from a Life at Disney*

*The Customer Rules: The 39 Essential Rules
for Delivering Sensational Service*

Introduction

I MET AMBER SEWELL in the modern sense: online.

Back in 2011, I ran a mega-site called Disney Dispatch. I had a few dozen weekly columnists, including Disney Legends like Rolly Crump, and I began to notice in my Google Analytics reports that one particular column was doing better than most of the other columns. In fact, it sometimes drew more traffic than Rolly Crump! Who wrote it?

Amber Sewell, of course.

I had pitched Amber the idea of a weekly column about her Disney CareerStart and Disney College Program adventures called Amber Earns Her Ears. I figured it would interest other College Program participants. But Amber threw herself heart and soul into the column, and her weekly "diary from Disney" drew faithful flocks of readers young and old.

Well before Amber finished the College Program, I sold Disney Dispatch, and most of the columnists left the site. Amber stuck around for a bit, but then she drifted off as well. Her diary? Unfinished.

About a year later, I got back in touch with Amber to ask whether she'd like to revise and expand her old Disney Dispatch columns, and write new material (lots of it!) to pick up from where she left off.

I told her we'd turn it into a book.

If you're not familiar with Disney CareerStart or the Disney College Program, don't worry: you'll learn about them right along with Amber.

I ought to mention that Disney discontinued CareerStart a couple of years ago. CareerStart and the College Program (which is still active and enrolls thousands of participants every year) are mostly identical, except that you could apply for CareerStart while still in high school. Once enrolled, however, participants in both programs take on the same Cast Member roles and duties.

In the first part of the book, Amber chronicles her semester in CareerStart, and then in the second part, she covers her semester in the College Program.

Want to follow in Amber's footsteps? If you're a college student, and if you'd like to spend your next semester in a theme park instead of in a classroom, maybe you can: http://disneycollegeprogram.com.

Enough with the preliminaries. Let's get to work — for Disney.

Bob McLain
Theme Park Press
April 2013

Part One

My First Semester at Walt Disney World

ON FEBRUARY 5, 2010, I pulled out of my driveway at two in the morning, my sister in the seat beside me and my parents in the car ahead. My car (affectionately known as Dinosaur) was packed to the brim with bedding, boxes, lamps, and clothes. There was an air of anticipation and new beginnings despite the early hour—the fresh breath of a new adventure.

When I reached the end of our little Tennessee back road, about to turn onto the highway for the 655-mile journey to Orlando, I set my iPod to my Disney playlist and selected "Go the Distance" from *Hercules*:

> *I have often dreamed,*
> *Of a far off place,*
> *Where a great warm welcome,*
> *Will be waiting for me.*

As young Hercules sang of finding the place where he belonged, my odometer rolled through the miles toward a far-off place of my own.

Rewind.

Since I was an infant, Disney and I have had an incredibly strong relationship. I spent countless hours in front of the television, the monotonous click of the VHS player a soothing background to whatever Disney movie captured my interest at the time. I slept with my stuffed, purring Nala and my family of Aristocats. I sang along with

Ariel and Meg, and dressed up as Esmeralda for Halloween. Then, in 1998, my family took our first vacation to Walt Disney World.

We were hooked.

That first taste of Disney magic was enough to ignite, well, an addiction. No matter how many trips we took (and there have been many—our current total is over fifty), the magic never diminished; there was always more to explore, more Hidden Mickeys to find.

So my next, natural step, once I became old enough, of course, was to look for an opportunity to work there.

And that's where this story starts.

Chapter One

Amber Chases CareerStart

MY CHANCE TO WORK at Walt Disney World, to become part of the magic not just as a guest but as a Cast Member, came in December 2008.

I had wandered into the college section of a popular online Disney fan forum. At first, I assumed it was just a place where college-aged individuals discussed Disney, but then I saw that most of the discussions were about something called the Disney College Program. Unfortunately, after some digging, I soon realized that this amazing experience was beyond my reach as a junior in high school.

Then I found a link to the Disney CareerStart Program.

I dug more. I learned all I could about CareerStart. I was eligible! Well, almost. I had to graduate from high school first. So I arranged to graduate a semester early, and filled out my CareerStart application. Now all I had to do was wait until September, the earliest I'd be able to send it in.

The Disney CareerStart Program *was* (past tense because Disney has discontinued it) much like the Disney College Program: a six-month internship with the Walt Disney Company either at the Disneyland Resort in Anaheim, California, or at Walt Disney World in Orlando, Florida.

By participating in CareerStart, I'd be able to move to Florida and live in Orlando, just minutes away from Disney property. (Disney owned the property where I'd be living, but it was outside the actual gates of Disney, in an area known as Little Lake Bryan.) I could work for them and get my foot in the door of the company that had had such a major impact on my life. All before I even set foot in college! It was perfect.

Through the official CareerStart website and the unofficial Disney fan forums, I learned more about the program. The more I learned, the more excited I became. (From here on, pretty much everything I write about CareerStart applies to the College Program as well.)

For six months, I could work at Walt Disney World in one of many different roles. I could be a hostess in the Haunted Mansion, scowling at guests as they clambered into their Doom Buggies. I could be responsible for cleaning up Fantasyland as I interacted with guests and helped them find their way in the mass of people who flock daily to Magic Kingdom. I could serve milkshakes at Disney's Hollywood Studios in front of the Rock 'n' Roller Coaster, sell children their first set of Mickey ears, or sit atop one of the high chairs by the sand-filled pool at the Beach Club, keeping an eye on people hurtling down the slide (okay, I couldn't do that last one as I can't swim, but it might be an option for you).

I didn't really care what role they gave me, as long as I got to wear that Disney nametag and introduce myself as a Cast Member.

Once you're accepted into the program, Disney provides almost everything necessary to live on your own in Florida.

For many participants, it's the first time living away from home, but Disney removes much of the anxiety and effort from that milestone event. They provide housing in one of four apartment complexes on the doorstep of Walt Disney World: Chatham Square, Patterson Court, The Commons, or Vista Way. Each complex has its own champions and detractors.

Patterson, the newest of the four complexes, is perhaps the nicest. It has a reputation as the quietest of the housing communities — some enjoy the silence, especially after a long day at work, but those craving a livelier atmosphere might not like it. Patterson is the only complex without a bus stop; it shares one with Chatham, which is just next door. Not a huge difference, but enough to discourage lazier individuals (such as myself) from staying there.

Vista Way is the oldest complex, and has developed quite a reputation.

Nicknamed "Vista Lay", it's the party complex, perfect for those who enjoy the most sociable atmosphere and the cheapest rent. But Vista isn't all bad. The buildings have recently undergone renovations, and security is always around to make sure the fun doesn't get out of hand.

Chatham Square is the happy medium between Patterson and Vista Way. With nicer rooms than Vista, and a more sociable atmosphere than Patterson, Chatham is a good choice for those not quite sure which type of setting they'd prefer. It also has the benefit of being directly across from Mickey's Retreat, a park for Cast Members that offers lakeside canoes and kayaks for rent, swimming pools, grills, and tennis and basketball courts.

The Commons is the fourth apartment complex, but it's restricted to program participants from abroad — the international students. I made several visits there, as many events and activities, such as grocery bingo and housing orientation, are held in the Commons' main building.

Living in a complex isn't free. Disney deducts the rent from your paycheck. How much they deduct depends on the number of roommates you have — apartments can accommodate two to eight people — and which complex you live in. The more people in the apartment, the cheaper the rent, and the newer the complex, the more expensive the rent.

Not only do the apartment complexes provide a place to live, they also feature swimming pools, gyms, tennis courts, a soccer field, 24-hour security, and limitless opportunities for fun: soccer tournaments, trips to the beach or theatre, baseball games, grocery bingo, and dozens of other amusements (not to mention the welcome parties for each incoming batch of participants). The initial payment you make to Disney upon your acceptance into the program covers the fees for all of these activities as well as your first week of rent.

Disney also provides buses (separate from those that transport guests) that take program participants to and from work, the parks (for which you get free admission!), and places like the grocery store, Walmart, the post office, and even the Florida Mall. Bringing a car may make some people more comfortable, but it's unnecessary. If you want to go somewhere the buses don't run, it's easy to find someone who'll take you there.

As if housing and transportation weren't enough, another valuable aspect of the program is the learning opportunities.

Disney offers classes designed by Cast Members who work for Disney University. From "Creativity and Innovation" and "Corporate Analysis" to "Marketing You", there is a class to capture anyone's interest.

Quite a few of these classes are ACE accredited, so many colleges will award credits. Check with your college advisor to make sure the credits will count, but even if they won't, the classes are interesting enough to attend for their own sake. You do have to buy the books and pay a minimal registration fee. If you take a course for credit, you'd also have to pay whatever tuition your college charges.

Networking is another overlooked program perk. Seminars, presentations by guest speakers, and numerous other opportunities for making valuable connections are easy to find, even if you're not exactly looking. For someone who wants to make a future with Disney, the program is an excellent way to begin. Whether it's chatting with managers about your aspirations, bumping into the head of tourism backstage in Magic Kingdom, or speaking to the vice president of your park as they drop by your restaurant, it's always possible to find ways to edge up in the company. My roommate and I learned this lesson when we were least expecting it — but that's a story for later.

The information I accumulated was enough to convince me beyond a shadow of a doubt that CareerStart was something I needed to do.

I was already graduating high school early, so taking a few more classes at a community college to make up for the time I'd be out of the classroom was a small price to pay for a semester in Walt Disney World and the chance to add an internship with a Fortune 100 company to my résumé.

But all that came later.

For now, I had nothing to do but wait until I could submit my application.

Chapter Two

Amber Sweats Her Interviews

A FEW MONTHS HAD passed since my initial fervor about the CareerStart Program. Somehow, I'd pushed it to the back of my mind as I made plans to take a Disney cruise or spend three weeks in England. In fact, I'd forgotten about CareerStart completely, and only an email from Disney about the obligatory ePresentation brought it back into focus.

There is remarkable magic in the word "Disney". Even the prospect of going to England for a school trip (I have wanted to go since I was at least ten years old) was eclipsed by an image of Mickey Mouse waving at me from my computer screen.

So, as much as I looked forward to a cruise and three weeks in England, I immediately put those plans aside.

The next day I viewed the CareerStart ePresentation — basically, a promotional video for the CareerStart and College Programs, where you'll hear about the many opportunities that await, watch squeaky clean tours of the housing complexes, and listen to cheesy, scripted interviews with past program participants.

I was hooked again.

Immediately, I pulled out the folder in which I had accumulated all of my information about CareerStart, including the all-important application. I looked over the application to make sure that I'd spelled every word correctly and punctuated everything just right. Then I went to school the next day and faxed it to Disney.

Had I bothered to check, I would have known that Disney now took applications online, and that they no longer required applicants to submit references or respond to short answer questions (of the sort "Why do you want to work for the company?" and "How did your previous work experience prepare you for Disney?").

Heedless, I faxed it all in, and then fell into the habit of obsessively checking my e-mail every ten minutes and stalking Disney fan sites to chat with other CareerStart hopefuls.

A few days passed — it might have even been a week or more — and I still hadn't heard from Disney about my application. I was starting to get nervous. Would I get rejected simply because I hadn't followed the rules? People had already done their phone interviews, and I hadn't heard so much as a squeak from Mickey.

Before panic could totally set in, I got an e-mail from Disney informing me that my application had, in fact, been received, and that I could proceed to the web interview.

I've heard horror stories about the web interview. People had been rejected just minutes after submitting their answers to the many questions on this totally automated test. Never had I felt more nervous than I did the morning I sat down in my high school's library during my free first period. I launched the CareerStart web interview and wriggled anxiously in my seat as the introductory page loaded. Taking a deep breath, I clicked "Proceed" and began.

It really was not all it had been talked up to be.

The CareerStart web interview was similar to programs used by employers to screen prospective employees. I was given a series of statements about my personality and work ethic (for example: "You prefer to work alone") and prompted to select one of five possible answers: "strongly disagree", "disagree", "neutral", "agree", or "strongly agree". All the questions were in this format, and all of them were relatively simple, even given the short time limit placed upon each response.

Putting myself into the mindset of a future Cast Member, I worked my way through the questions, always trying to select one of the strong options, and very rarely choosing neutral. I stuck to the truth, though. I know a lot of people are tempted to exaggerate qualities that they think companies want, but in my case, I really do want some time alone after I've been surrounded by people for hours.

It took me thirty or forty minutes to finish the web interview. My reward? The marvelous little message telling me that I had passed. I scribbled down the number I would have to call to schedule my phone interview and raced to the secretary's office where I would be able to use my cell phone to make the call. Hands trembling, adrenaline rushing, I called Disney and wrote down the time of my phone interview, then headed back to the library to spend more time in Disney chat rooms before my next class.

Now that I had passed the web interview, I began to prepare for the phone interview.

I read other people's experiences, and wandered through the halls of my high school thinking, "What would I say to a child who's too small to ride Space Mountain?"

I had read somewhere that it was a good idea to ask some questions after the interview, just to show that I was really involved and had done lots of Disney research. The problem was that actually I *had* researched everything, and so I had no questions. I scribbled down a few queries anyway, despite already knowing the answers.

I had scheduled my interview for another free morning at school. I forewarned my second period teacher that I might be late (she, of course, was almost as excited as I was), and then on the day of the interview, I went outside and sat on a bench to await Disney's call. My notes and application were spread out on the ground all around me, some weighted down with pebbles. I nervously kept checking my phone, watching every minute pass by with excruciating slowness.

Finally, the time for my interview arrived.

There was no call. My stomach clenched as I waited for the phone to ring. A minute passed; then another. Instead of a ring, my phone began to vibrate. I had a voicemail.

With dread, I quickly entered my password and listened as my interviewer explained that the call had not gone through, and she would try calling back in just a few minutes.

I hung up, staring around as if the reason my phone hadn't rang was hidden behind one of the cars in the parking lot. Not knowing what else to do, I called my mother, pacing nervously. After I had explained everything in a barely coherent rush, she said that I had probably been sitting in an odd spot where there was no service. I was at the foot of a mountain, after all, where service isn't entirely reliable. This did nothing to calm my nerves — what if it happened again? What if Disney was never able to get through, and marked me down as ignoring their call?

But just then the phone began to vibrate once more. I quickly hung up with my mom and answered the phone.

My interviewer (I regret to say that I don't remember her name, though she was incredibly personable and lovely to chat with) pushed aside my apologies and quickly put me at ease. As soon as I was sure that I wasn't going to be in trouble for not getting the first call, I was able to relax and do what I do best: chat about Disney.

I thoroughly enjoyed the phone interview. Of course I was nervous, tracing the cracks in the sidewalk as I paced, but all of the preparation I had done was completely unnecessary.

First, we reviewed my application, verifying that all the information was correct.

Then came another scare. I was still seventeen and in high school, although I was taking three college courses as well. Apparently, this had come off as confusing on paper, and my interviewer asked if I would rather apply to the College Program.

After a few minutes of bewildering conversation, we were finally able to clarify my position — which ended up being questionable. The interviewer triple-checked my birth date, then put me on hold for a few minutes to make sure that my 18th birthday would come prior to my arrival in Orlando for CareerStart — one of the program's non-negotiable requirements.

I agonized for a few minutes, and then she was back, having confirmed that there were, in fact, a few arrival dates in February past my birthday.

Now the real interview began.

I was asked why I wanted to work for the company: simple, I have been in love with it since infancy. How might my previous work experience have prepared me for situations that might arise in Disney?

I worked at the local animal clinic as both a secretary and an assistant for eight years, so I had an varied skill set that would apply to many situations, and not just those involving animals. I emphasized my cash-handling experience because, for a lot of CareerStart participants, this could be their first time working in retail (not everyone in the program works in retail, but some do). Prior experience always puts you on better ground.

The interviewer asked me a few more generic questions, and then came the Disney ones.

What would I do if I saw a guest spill their drink? I replied that I would immediately put up a sign to caution other guests, and then clean the spill myself (only afterward did I realize I also should have given the guest something else to drink). I emphasized that since Disney is full of children, and children like to run, it wouldn't do for them to slip in someone's spilled beverage and hurt themselves. I was asked the traditional Space Mountain question as well, and then to list my favorite parks and rides.

After a little more chatting, we hung up.

My phone interview had lasted 46 minutes; some people finish theirs in 15 minutes. I wasn't worried, though, because a lot of my interview time had been spent chatting about wherever my last answer led: from people's attachments to animals to the view at the Beach Club.

After another quick chat with Mom (mothers like to stay updated about these things, and I needed to get some of the excess adrenaline out of my system), I went to World Geography — where all of my excess energy was immediately drained by an educational video.

Thus began one of the longest waits of my life.

Chapter Three

Amber Hates the Wait

"HAVE YOU CHECKED THE mail today?" my Dad asked me.

"No! I mean, yes, I've checked, but that doesn't mean you're allowed to."

"So nothing from the Mouse yet?"

"Dad, if I'd heard from Disney, I think the entire world would know by now."

Never had I been so diligent about anything. My CareerStart interviewer told me that Disney would contact me in one of three ways: by e-mail, by phone, or by snail mail.

I was going crazy, constantly checking all three. My computer screen was always open to my e-mail while at school, and I double-checked it at home on my cell phone (rather than wrestle with the evil that is dial-up). Only *I* was allowed to retrieve the mail from the mailbox, and I constantly grabbed for the phone when it rang, looking for a 407 (Orlando) area code or the official number for Disney's CareerStart.

I couldn't be separated from Disney fan sites, either. I shared my wait with dozens of other hopefuls; I even joined a Facebook group of the most devoted applicants. We discussed everything from how we passed the time to what classes we hoped to take if (*when*) we were accepted. One of the members sent me an invite to "like" the Electric Umbrella's page; it saddens me to say that I didn't recognize the name (though in my defense, I have a rule to eat only in the World Showcase when in EPCOT, and Electric Umbrella is a quick-service restaurant in Future World), but it was Disney, so I accepted.

Two weeks passed.

Disney had told some applicants that they'd hear back within 2-3 weeks (those were the optimists). Others were told 3-4 weeks (the most common response), and some unfortunate souls were told that their agony could last up to 6 weeks. We all fervently hoped we were not in the last group.

I annoyed my family and friends daily. The only topic I seemed able to discuss was Disney. I talked about the parks, about how I was going absolutely crazy waiting to hear back, the amazing things I'd heard from past participants, what role I wanted, where I wanted to work, and much, much more. I'm fairly certain that sometimes I even got on my own nerves; honestly, couldn't I think of anything else to talk about?

Clearly not.

Of course, not everyone was hoping I'd get accepted. My co-workers at the animal clinic weren't too enthused at the prospect of me leaving; I had been there for a long time, and knew a lot of stuff that would not be fun training others to do. There was even talk of cloning me, or giving false bad references to Disney. While it was all in jest (or at least, I think most of it was), I did attempt to moderate my enthusiasm when at the clinic. I'm not saying that it worked, but at least I made the effort.

At three weeks I was starting to get nervous. I was seventeen, after all. Even though I have an excess of enthusiasm for Disney, I thought that my age might be my potential downfall. I didn't think I said anything wrong in my interview, but I kept going over that first five minutes, when my interviewer had put me on hold to check the arrival dates. Did the recruiters take age into account? Surely they did.

Seventeen...

It sounded awfully young to move to Florida by myself. Perhaps they didn't think I would be able to handle it. Maybe they thought the work would be too much for me, and I would quit and go home. What if they lumped me with other teenagers they knew, the ones who are more likely to text on the job than actually learn something? If I called them after I'd been rejected, would they give me an honest answer?

All I could do was wait. I couldn't speed up the process (as much as I would have liked), and there was no number I could call to convince Disney that just because my birthday was only two weeks before move-in, I would still work hard.

So I continued to check the mail. I kept my e-mail open. I spent my time in journalism class quickly proofreading others' articles for the newspaper or writing something of my own, and then it was back to the Disney sites.

My anxiety was a convenient source of agitation for my family. Not that I blame them; I would probably have done the same thing. Sometimes the mail truck would supposedly come two or three times in a day, usually at the most inconvenient times for me. Usually, I brushed them off; didn't they think I had made a point to figure out when the mail came?

One of these times I was in the shower, and my dad knocked on the door.

"Have you checked the mail today?"

"Um, yeah. I checked it a little while ago. There wasn't anything there."

"Well, I just saw the mailman. He may have had something for you."

As much as I tried to ignore this hint, just as I had all the others, my excitement built despite my suspicions. I have a long driveway, and just watching me walk it up and down is enough to amuse my family. I'm not exactly the active type.

I threw on some sweat pants and an "I 'Heart' Grumpy Guys" T-shirt, slipped into some flip flops, and went down to check the mail. It was all I could do not to run. The knowledge that my family would be watching from the window was enough to keep me at walking pace.

As soon as I got past the bushes that would block me from view, I sprinted the last few feet, crossed the road, and wrenched open our old, battered mail box.

There it was.

My beautiful, large envelope with Mickey Mouse standing in the top left corner. My name was on the front. Just the size of the envelope was reassuring; it was big enough to fit a yellow folder (the universal sign of acceptance for the CareerStart Program; the College Program uses purple folders).

Forgetting that I loathe running, or that my driveway is basically uphill, or that by now my entire family would be watching because Dad had told them that my folder was in the mail (the mailman had actually tried to give Dad the mail, but he made him put my envelope back in the mailbox so I could retrieve it), I rushed up the driveway.

Probably not the wisest thing on my part, because it took me a few minutes to catch my breath after I finally made it back into the living room. I lay on the floor, surrounded by everyone, as I tried to breathe normally and sit up. Eventually, I did, and with hands shaking from adrenaline, I tore open the envelope.

There it was.

Orange-yellow in color, "Disney CareerStart" printed in bold across the front. I was holding the key to a new world.

Beaming, I opened the folder and read aloud my acceptance letter.

Dear Amber:

Congratulations! You have been selected to participate as a Quick-Service Food & Beverage Cast Member on the Disney CareerStart Program for the Spring 2010 Season!

Chapter Four

Amber Picks Her Roomies

THE SMELL OF COFFEE filled the air. My sister, Hayley, and I sat in our regular spot: a small table by the window, watching passersby as they entered Barnes & Noble. As I sipped my berry soda and watched Hayley take the first bite of her sandwich — an odd creation made with turkey and apples — I ran through my mental checklist of the many things still to accomplish before the start of my Florida adventure.

As soon as I recovered from my dash up the driveway and the shock of my acceptance into Disney's CareerStart Program, one of the first things I did was write a shopping list of all the items I would need for living on my own.

Here, again, Disney fan sites and fellow participants proved their usefulness.

Disney's official CareerStart site offered a general list of necessary items like bedding, televisions, Ethernet cables, and business attire. I was more than happy to copy it down. Past participants also gave their advice as to exactly how much to pack (naturally, I failed to follow that advice), and those who had also just been accepted into the program feverishly debated such essential questions as whether we should buy shower curtains and hangers before we left, or wait until we arrived and hope the stores hadn't run out.

Another quandary quickly arose: we had been accepted, yes, but our shopping wouldn't be just for ourselves. What would our roommates think of our personal taste in decorations, tablecloths, and bath mats?

Some people chose to let fate select their roommates. They would arrive in Florida blind, knowing no one and having no clue as to who they would be living with for the next four or six months (College Programmers have the option of a shorter program, lasting just four months).

Others knew exactly where they hoped to live, how many bedrooms they were going to have, and who would sleep in those beds.

I wasn't quite sure which path to follow.

The thing about choosing a roommate is that you never really know a person until you meet them. You can chat all you want on the internet, but until you meet face-to-face, it's difficult to judge whether you'll get along. If it turned out that I couldn't get along with my roommates, I could request that Disney move me into another apartment — but that entailed a $50 fee and possibly hurt feelings or a nasty farewell scene.

I felt it better to arrive not knowing anyone. Sure, I'd be taking a chance, but not much more than if I had arranged to room with someone I'd never physically met. So I decided to let fate decide. I'd stand in line at check-in, strike up a conversation with the people around me, and select on the spot the people I'd be living with for the next six months.

Roommate surveys dominated the online forums. People sent private messages and exchanged cell phone numbers, trying to gauge compatibility. I answered the generic questions and sent sporadic messages, but only half-heartedly. While I'd have liked to arrange the color scheme of the bathroom, or how many televisions would be in the apartment, it wasn't something that dominated my thoughts. And I'm a fairly introverted person by nature; the idea of striking up a conversation with a complete stranger and asking whether they were interested in becoming a roommate? Not my idea of fun.

So I continued to shop. I had a list of things to buy, categorized either as "personal" or "room", all color-coded with different pens. When I bought an item, I checked it off my list and then stored it in one of the green tubs that now lined a section of my room.

Weekends became shopping expeditions, usually in the company of my younger sister. With the windows down and music playing loudly, I would drive us the forty-five minutes to the shopping center where we would patrol the aisles of Target accumulating towels, washcloths, an iron, plates, and cups. Even the most mundane items were exciting, as they symbolized the beginning of an amazing exploit.

Our trips would inevitably end with a visit to Barnes & Noble, where we'd sit in the little café and eat a late lunch during which Hayley would try to talk me out of buying yet another book, and I would usually override her logic. We'd talk of my plans for Florida, the general air of excitement, the things that I had yet to buy. It was a nice little ritual we established before I moved away.

Christmas came in the midst of everything, and with it a vast array of things to take with me: a mini ironing board, a coffee maker (the most essential purchase), and a dozen other useful items.

I told what I knew about the program to countless friends and family members, sometimes multiple times if they were in the habit of forgetting things.

And each time I told it, my excitement grew.

The days were creeping by: a few weeks before, I had finally graduated from high school, and now I spent much of my time at the animal clinic, working as many hours as possible before I'd have to leave for good.

One day, as I was meandering through my favorite unofficial Disney fan site, I saw that I had a private message from someone named Paige, a girl who'd seen my roommate survey on the College Board forum. We had a lot of things in common, she pointed out, including our favorite show, *Gilmore Girls*. Anyone who liked *Gilmore Girls*, she wrote, couldn't be all bad. I looked her up on Facebook, and after a few more messages, we agreed to be roommates. So much for letting fate decide!

After the initial conversation, we didn't really talk much. I was too daunted by the awkwardness of getting to know a stranger online to initiate conversations — after all, what would I say? So I let it lie; we had common interests, and that would give us things to discuss once we arrived in Orlando. I was fine with that.

Later, two other girls from Facebook, Violet and Rebecca, asked to stay with us. We agreed, and we all chatted back and forth for a while. But it was still a long time before we would move, and conversation lapsed again. The only other thing Paige and I discussed before arriving was the color scheme for our bathroom — green and blue.

Honestly, I didn't exert much energy in planning for my move to Florida.

Most of the things I bought were common-sense items for anyone moving anywhere and starting from scratch. As much as I loved my family, I had been formulating these kinds of lists for years. Some things I bought for fun — brownie mix, for example — but most of it was practical. I knew I was going to be taking my car, and that Disney would provide a parking space. I had picked out my roommates, knew there was a Target near the apartment complexes, and made some acquaintances who'd be starting the program along with me. Our Facebook group planned a dinner the night prior to check-in for us to meet and say hello. I wasn't sure if I would go or not, but at least it was an option.

So, as the day of departure drew nearer, and my shopping list dwindled to stray items, the surreal nature of my situation slowly began to dissolve. Not that it ever left, really, but it began to sink in that I was doing this.

As I packed up Dinosaur on my last day at home, shoving boxes behind seats and shifting my bag of books so the trunk would close, I thought to myself with a smile that by this time next week, I would be an official Disney Cast Member.

And that was something to be excited about.

Chapter Five

Amber Drives to Disney World

"I HOPE YOU'RE GONNA be able to stay awake for the entire drive down," Dad told me smugly, staring at the bulky cardboard box containing my bedding shoved behind the driver's seat. "Because there is no way that I'm going to be able to fit in your car."

It was true. Dinosaur had been crammed full of supplies (quite literally—I was lucky any of the doors shut), and it was time to get some rest before starting the lovely eleven-hour drive to Florida.

Despite my excitement, I knew I'd need some sleep to prepare for that drive. So we all went to bed early, alarms set for the ungodly hour of 1:30 a.m.

All too soon, the alarms went off.

In a stupor, we stumbled about the house, changing into our comfortable driving clothes and triple-checking that we had everything we needed before stepping out into the chilly East Tennessee morning, pairing up into our cars, and starting down the driveway.

That first hour was full of tense excitement. My playlist of favorite Disney songs filled Dino with an appropriate, optimistic Disney vibe. My sister, Hayley, was awake, the stars were out, and I was on my way.

I have always loved driving at night. There's a silence to the landscape that the sun manages to burnish away, and it seemed fitting to start my journey in such an anticipatory manner. It was this peaceful atmosphere, however, that lulled my assistant driver to sleep.

The entire purpose of Hayley coming with us (my brothers were staying with relatives) was to keep me awake on the drive. As the early morning progressed, and as I turned up the volume of the radio higher and higher (my strategy was to sing the entire way down — who can fall asleep when singing?), she lay back in the seat, mouth half open, utterly useless.

I think I listened to every type of music on the way to Florida. I started with Disney music, then moved to Norah Jones and Michael Bublé. After that came Paramore and Coldplay, the soundtrack from *Spring Awakening* and *The Last Five Years*. Whatever I thought had the potential to keep me awake, I played.

On our many previous trips to Disney World, I was always the one most likely to be awake at any given moment. What I hadn't counted on, however, was my inability to change positions. I envied Hayley in the seat beside me — not only because she was asleep but because she was able to curl up, stretch out, and contort her body to relieve the discomfort of being in a small space for an extended period of time. I didn't have that luxury.

I don't remember if we stopped for breakfast. No one in my family really considers it a meal — a cup of coffee is usually enough at such an early hour. Besides, we had stocked each car with a few snacks to munch on throughout the day. The less stops we made, the quicker we would get to Disney World.

I am not the best of drivers even under good circumstances; I get incredibly nervous when driving somewhere new. And cities? Well, let's just say I had little to no experience driving through those.

When we reached Atlanta, a massive thunderstorm was underway. I love the rain. I'm usually not opposed to driving in it. But that dark morning, I would have given anything for it to stop. I remember reaching over to punch Hayley awake, because there was no way I was going to be the only one in that car panicking. Mom was driving the car in front of us, which I thought was a good thing. Of my parents, she is the more … cautious driver, I suppose.

I was wrong.

Seventy miles an hour. In the rain. I hydroplaned at least thirty-five times; I kept count. It was the one time in the trip when the music was barely audible — my nerves were frayed enough, and I didn't need any extraneous noise to snap them.

Any time an exit ramp came up, I panicked. Atlanta was the one place on previous trips where I'd usually take a nap, and so I didn't know the route. I was lucky just to be able to see my mother's car in front of me. Maybe that's everyone's experience driving through Atlanta. Maybe hydroplaning really isn't that big a deal. But for a nervous, stressed-out 18 year old whose urban driving experience was limited to much smaller Knoxville? I was not enjoying it.

Eventually, we made it out.

The music came back on, Hayley fell asleep once more, and drained of energy, I struggled to stay awake. We stopped to get some caffeine — which doesn't really help my mother or me stay awake, but just seems like a good idea — and then drove on.

Around Perry, Georgia, we stopped at Chick-fil-A for lunch, a respite for which I was desperately grateful. I love my Dinosaur, but I really did not want to climb back in for another few hours.

But I did. The closer we got to Florida, the more exhausted I became. We ran into patches of rain, and other times the sun would shine down on us, filling the air with a smothering, sticky heat. Finally, we crossed the Florida state line, rolled down the windows, and opened the sunroof.

Dad was driving the lead car, and he wasn't fond that I tended to get distracted, sometimes not maintaining a steady distance between his car and mine. My state of exhaustion probably didn't help, either.

About an hour or two from Disney, I began to nod. I tried every trick in the book to stay awake — loud music, windows down, constantly shifting positions. Hayley, as she had done the entire trip, slept. Eventually, after a few close calls, the bouts of drowsiness passed, the last of the rain clouds evaporated, and signs for Orlando began to appear.

A few minutes from Disney World, Hayley finally woke up. She broke out the camera to document the last few miles of the journey, taking photos of the Orlando exit ramp and the sign telling us the short distance to Disney World.

And finally, the gates.

I followed Mom and Dad to Disney's Old Key West Resort, where we would be staying for a few nights before my CareerStart check-in. As we pulled up to the security gate and the guard welcomed us home, an enormous smile broke out on my face. I was here. (And there was a bed in the room!)

A nap was the first order of the day. Afterward, we got up and hit the parks. It was just like any other vacation, minus my brothers.

On February 7, I got texts from a few people who had also just arrived. The meet-n-greet dinner was still on at Downtown Disney: was I coming?

The idea of going to Downtown Disney by myself to meet a bunch of strangers held scant appeal. I'm not a social person; I prefer the company of a good book over a large group of strangers. True, one of my goals in participating in this program was to improve my social skills, but technically the program hadn't started yet. So, rather than meet my potential roommates, friends, and co-workers, I stayed in the hotel room and double-checked that I had everything ready for the morning.

I had the address of Vista Way (where I would be checking in), my folder, my car insurance information, passport, and driver's license. I ironed my clothes for the next day, and then fell into the bed to read myself to sleep.

Chapter Six

Amber Digs Her Disney Digs

FLORIDA IS NOT SUPPOSED to be cold.

On the morning of check-in, my parents, sister, and I were some of the first people to gather inside the security tent in front of Vista Way. Luckily, as early arrivals, we were able to commandeer the space next to the heater.

Rather than socialize, my timidity and I stayed near the heater, observing people from a safe distance. I pointed out Rebecca, one of my roommates: "That girl with the Mickey Mouse jacket is one of them," I told my mother. Except that it wasn't Rebecca; obviously, I hadn't spent much time studying my future roommates online. I recognized a few online acquaintances from their profile pictures, including Alex, a guy who had a huge interest in theatre, and who stood a head above everyone else in the tent.

Paige and I had been texting throughout the morning. She was running a little late, and wouldn't show up until it was almost time to check in. It appeared that a lot of people had made connections at the introductory dinner the previous night, and I felt the smallest twinge of regret over my decision not to go. Not a lot, though, as I was still a little intimidated by the mass of people around me. Little clusters of future Cast Members formed, despite the rather cramped space. I began to get anxious about my socializing ability; shouldn't I be over there, with the other participants? But my concern wasn't enough to cause me to leave the heater and join a conversation.

Eventually, another girl noticed that I was standing in the warm, orange glow and came to join me. We struck up a conversation, discussing our roles and where we hoped to live. She was a "friend of

Tigger", and neither of us really knew or cared which complex we lived in, as long as it wasn't Vista Way.

After a while, as the sun began to shine more brightly and the tent had filled to bursting, it was time to head toward the check-in building at the back of the complex. I waved goodbye to my parents and sister as they went to the parents' tent to wait for me and drink some hot chocolate.

Just before we started to move, I heard a squeal and was taken completely by surprise when I found myself on the receiving end of an enthusiastic hug. Paige had made it! Shorter than me, with dark frizzy hair and exuberant energy, Paige looked similar to the photo I had seen of her. We joined the throng of people slowly moving farther into the complex, and on the way struck up a conversation with two girls, Jenni and Leah, whom Paige had met at last night's gathering at Earl of Sandwich in Downtown Disney. Both of these girls were also shorter than me, with short brown hair and broad grins. (Leah, in fact, was the girl in the Mickey Mouse jacket I had earlier mistaken for Rebecca!) The air of excitement was tangible. We didn't know what we were about to do, we didn't know where we were going, but we couldn't wait to get started.

That cold February morning was a blur of paperwork, trivia questions, music, and loud chatter. I remember standing in line to go into a large building at the back of Vista when Jenni and I overheard someone talking about name tags. We immediately flew into a frenzy, wondering if we were about to receive our official Disney name tags already. It turned out the people we overheard were merely talking about temporary stick-ons, but we had no difficulty redirecting our enthusiasm.

After receiving our sticky name tags, we moved around the building to a side pavilion where a DJ was set up in the front, playing music and calling out trivia questions. People were constantly running up to receive prizes for their correct answers. After waiting in line, the four of us huddled around a table to fill out some paperwork, then we moved into the building where the main activity seemed to be taking place.

The first thing we did was tell the Disney Housing staff who we were going to room with, and in which complex we wanted to stay.

Paige took control of our little group. The two girls, Rebecca and Violet, that we had agreed to room with beforehand were lost in the sea of people behind us in line. Since Leah and Jenni had no one else to room with, we made a spontaneous decision to room together.

It was quite possibly the best decision I made for the entire six months.

To further our luck, Vista Way wasn't an option for the latest arrivals. Chatham or Patterson were left, both of which were wonderful choices. After a minute or two of "I don't care," and "me either", Paige told the Cast Member with the clipboard that we would room in Chatham.

As we waited for confirmation, we chatted with a group of boys from our Facebook group behind us in line; they had decided to room at Patterson. We joked about the perks of our respective complexes, and then Paige waved us over to join another line where we were assigned a two-bedroom apartment in Chatham, received our keys, and sat down to take a photo for our housing ID, the small plastic cards responsible for getting past Chatham security and onto the College Program buses (both programs used the same buses). Good luck getting the bus driver to let you on if you accidentally leave your ID on the coffee table — or even getting security to let you back in to retrieve it.

Once outside, I spotted the table for car registrations. Jenni and Leah had forgotten their insurance information, so they headed back to their cars to get it. We all agreed to meet up at the apartment — 22301! — when we were done with check-in.

I stayed at the little desk and struggled to understand the significance of the different papers in my folder. There was some question as to whether my name was actually on the insurance, but after a moment's digging, I unearthed a page with my name on it. I received a sticker to put on the lower left windshield of Dinosaur and two sheets of neon orange paper (one for Dinosaur, one for my parent's car) that would enable us to get past security and move everything into my new apartment.

After I rejoined my parents and Hayley at the tent, we walked back to the parking lot, climbed into our cars, and followed the directions to Chatham Square.

I was the first of the roommates to arrive. Up on the third floor, in a building at the back of the complex, I wandered through the rooms and, at my mother's encouragement, chose the one with the biggest closet. Then I began the many trips back and forth, up and down the stairs, carrying large plastic bins, paper bags, and an assortment of containers. For the most part, I just stacked everything up in the room to be put away later.

22301 was a nice little apartment — much more than I had been expecting from the pictures and videos. You walked in the door, and immediately to the left was Jenni and Leah's bathroom, which then led to their bedroom. A step farther brought you to a desk where the internet cables were set up. The spacious kitchen, complete with a double sink, dishwasher, stove, oven, fridge, and pantry, was on the right, with a dinner table close by. Our sizeable living room was on the left, furnished with a couch and chairs, a coffee table, and a smaller table where we'd put someone's TV. Part of the room behind the living room furniture looked as if the architects had thought about putting in a balcony, then changed their minds. We weren't quite sure what to do with that space, and it came to be referred to as our useless nook. Then at the far end of the room was the bedroom, bathroom, and closet that I'd share with Paige.

When the other girls arrived, I helped carry in their things while our parents chatted in the kitchen. Finally, when everything had been moved in (I thought I had brought a lot, but Leah arrived with a U-Haul trailer in tow; admittedly, though, she did drive a Bug), we sat down on the couch and took our first roommate picture.

After our parents, with many hugs, had dispersed, we began to unpack and get to know one another a bit before walking over to the Commons for our first housing meeting which was, as per usual with these kinds of things, rather dull. There were grand efforts to make it entertaining , and the guy from Housing almost succeeded in keeping our attention for most of it. From stories about a linebacker tackling a roommate who pulled a prank on him involving a fake sword to the cheesy videos informing us of the different services offered by the complexes, he did manage to elicit a few peals of laughter from the crowd.

As soon as he left, the monotonous listing of rules began, and my interest plummeted. Despite the decorations shown hanging on apartment walls in the ePresentation video, the only thing you can hang are corkboards (and only the corkboards provided for you). You can't open the windows. You must wear your ID at all times, and if you don't have it, good luck getting into the complex. You can't sleep in someone else's apartment. You can't drink if you're underage. You can't smoke in the apartment. And so forth.

Every few months, Housing would inspect the apartments for cleanliness. They would post the inspection date for your apartment building on a sign by the bus stop and at the security gate. At some unspecified time during that day, you'd hear a knock on your door. If you sleep through the knock, or don't hear it because you're in the shower, you'd hear a loud whistle and the sound of your door being unlocked as a team of three inspectors enter the apartment and begin to check bathrooms, trash cans, sinks, walls, carpets — anything you can mess up, they'll check it, and if they find particularly egregious infractions of the rules, they'll photograph them as evidence. If your apartment fails the inspection, Disney will deduct $25 from each roommate's next paycheck to cover the cost of a cleaning crew.

The speaker made a point to explain which rules were a little more flexible — you're not going to be kicked out the first time they find you at someone else's apartment, or if you're underage at an apartment where others are drinking. But it is, after all, Disney, and the Disney Image has to be protected.

Once the lengthy seminar was over, we walked back to our apartment, where my parents were waiting to take me to Walmart to stock up on groceries and other necessities. By the time we reached Walmart, however, I was exhausted. Not just exhausted, but in that state of exhaustion where everything is funny, and even the hint of having to make a decision causes your eyes to tear up in frustration. The excitement of the morning had worn off, leaving me sapped of any energy or thinking ability. As we meandered through the aisles, Mom kept suggesting things to buy, and I kept giving noncommittal answers. By the next morning, I was regretting my inattention, and realized that I should have bought more food. But all I had been able to think about in Walmart was my new bed in my new home.

Finally, my parents dropped me off at the apartment with my scant groceries, and I said goodbye — at least for a little while. They were staying until I got my assignment and learned what kind of shoes I would need. I would get that information, and much more, a few days later at Traditions.

Chapter Seven

Amber Learns the Disney Way

THE DOORKNOBS WERE SHAPED like the ones in *Alice in Wonderland*. The hallways were painted with Disney characters. Ramps led up and down, random corridors branched off to unknown locations, and a bunch of young adults in varying states of business attire stood clustered together, gazing around with a uniform look of bemused anticipation.

That was my first—and lasting—impression of Casting. Luckily, Paige, Leah, Jenni, and I all got along wonderfully, so we clung together as much as possible before they put us in alphabetical order and marched us, a little shell-shocked, through the business side of Disney—a side we hadn't seen before. Yes, Paige had worked at a Disney Store in Washington, D.C. prior to joining the program, but this was different from a stock room in a mall.

A bus had come to our complex early that morning to take us to Casting, where we would receive our work locations, submit fingerprints, and complete the myriad other tasks required for us to become Cast Members. We walked in—past the doorknobs, which held us up for a bit as pictures were taken—and joined lines of other new CareerStart participants strung through a hallway. We didn't have a clue what we were doing, other than following orders. When word passed down the line that we were about to learn where we would be working for the next six months, a murmur of excited chatter arose.

As I queued up and got closer to the desk where people were getting stickers plastered onto their College Program booklets (already, CareerStart had ceased to exist; once you've finally made it to Florida, the two programs function the same way, so even though I was technically in the CareerStart Program, all the training and introductory materials were identical to that used for the College Program), my mind was racing with possibilities. I had already decided the most preferable spot would be the shake stand just outside Rock 'n' Roller Coaster; what better way to spend the day than listening to Aerosmith? Maybe then I would finally learn all the words. The smiling Cast Member took my folder and applied my sticker. Breathless, I looked down:

Electric Umbrella.

Electric Umbrella?

Honestly, I remembered Electric Umbrella only from a link someone on Facebook had sent me. I couldn't remember ever eating there, and I wasn't even sure where it was (a rare occurrence), but that didn't matter. I was working at Disney World!

As I waited in another line to be inspected for compliance with the Disney Look, I hurriedly sent out a text to my mother, letting her know that I was working in EPCOT. Then, as the line advanced, I shoved my phone back in my purse and peered ahead to see what was happening.

In groups of four, we were inspected by a Cast Member who assessed our hair color, clothes, tattoos (if we had any), jewelry, and every other aspect of our appearance to ensure that we complied with the Disney Look. While the rules for the Look have slackened over time, the guidelines for College Program participants are quite strict. Hair had to be of a natural color, with no roots showing if it was dyed. Men's facial hair was compared to a few charts the Cast Members had on hand, clothes were assessed for level of appropriateness, and even nails were checked to ensure they were of a proper length. Luckily, no one in our group had any problems, but I have heard of people who had to go home and dye their hair before they did anything else, or buy special make-up to cover their tattoos. Disney posts the Disney Look guidelines on the College Program website, so it's easy (and advisable) to log in and make sure you qualify ahead of time.

More tedious tasks ensued. We were taken through a string of offices to fill out more paperwork and answer more questions. Adding our fingerprints to the system proved to be troublesome — my thumb was refusing to scan, and I wasn't the only one having issues. Leah encountered a plethora of problems with the business side of Disney, beginning with the background check. It took aeons to process, and she wasn't able to start training until later than the rest of us.

Eventually, though, it was almost over. We queued up for one last room, where we received even more booklets and rules, and then picked up our debit cards. Once we registered the cards, we'd be sent a text whenever money (such as our Disney paychecks, which were deposited every Thursday) was put on them, and whenever money was spent. I eventually switched over to the Partners Federal Credit Union, a Cast Member banking system with an office located just down the road from Chatham and Patterson, and another at Disney University.

As people trickled out, I found a seat on a bench outside to wait for Jenni, Paige, and Leah so we could all ride a bus back to our apartment together. One by one the others emerged, pausing to take pictures with the costumed characters that Disney had waiting for us at the exit.

On the bus back, we all compared Traditions times, which were on the sticker that told us where we would be working. Jenni and I had Traditions together; Leah, sadly, wouldn't get to attend Traditions until later, due to the delay with her background check (we never did find out what took so long). Back at the apartment, we retired to our seats in the living room — everyone had already picked out their spots — and chatted, getting to know each other more. Now that we were evolving out of that awkward strangers phase, personalities were starting to emerge.

Jenni was the comedian. Everything was funny when she was around, and every night would end with all four of us collapsed in hopeless laughter in the living room over some outrageous comment she had made. Many inside jokes emerged from late night conversations — late being somewhere around ten, when things took a definite turn from fairly normal to absolutely nonsensical.

Leah was compassionate, creative, and fun-loving. She was quite the seamstress, too. While the rest of our rooms had a slightly lived-in feel (except for Jenni's room, since she never did manage to unpack everything she had brought), Leah's assortment of knick-knacks — from pillows she had made and then thrown on the couch to picture frames everywhere — made the apartment feel like a home in no time.

Paige was more logical and down-to-earth, with a drier sense of humor that I totally appreciate. She was a gamer, and the biggest Disney fan I had ever met. Her goal was to be a tour guide for the Keys to the Kingdom tour — anything we needed to know about anything Disney, she was our source of information. She was also a huge Harry Potter fan, which meant that we were destined to have a few adventures on that front.

And I fit in quietly, still warming up to everything. I got incredibly lucky, standing next to those three in line on check-in day. They made it easier for me to meet my goal of becoming more sociable; there was no awkward tip-toeing around, no arguing over fridge or pantry space, no complaining about sinks full of dishes or the air conditioner being on too high. After that first night, we had all become friends.

The days before and after Traditions were filled with relaxation and getting to know people. My parents came by again, and we went to the outlets to buy some black, no-slip tennis shoes for the Electric Umbrella. We also picked up a houseguest for 22301 — Alex, the theatre fan from our Facebook group. He and Jenni had become friends before the program, and his goofy personality fit in well with the rest of us.

Alex also had Traditions the same day as Jenni and me. As the day rolled around, I slipped into a skirt and button-down, then walked with Jenni to the bus stop in the chilly morning air. There we were greeted by plenty of other CareerStart and College Programmers in various states of business attire. We found Alex and one of his roommates, and stood clustered together, waiting for the bus. Other CPs, already well into their program, lounged on benches or stood with headphones attached, waiting for their buses to take them to work, hardly sparing a glance at the bunch of newcomers. Finally, the bus with a "Traditions" sign in the front window rolled around, and we piled on.

Traditions was ... amazing. It was a day of Disney history, games, videos, and tours. Alex, Jenni, and I sat at the same table, and slowly a few others joined us. We wrote our names on our Disney course books, and slapped yet another sticky nametag onto our chests.

I have been told that Traditions changes a lot. I'm not sure which aspects change, but I do know that I had goose bumps as we watched the introductory video, which featured clips of people's enthusiasm for the company, guests' reactions, Art the doorman at the Beach Club (who no longer works there), and testimonials by Cast Members about working at Disney. A lot of people who participate in the program have never visited Disney World — Jenni, for instance, as well as many of the Cast Members from other countries — and Traditions does an excellent job of introducing strangers to this new and complex world.

A cheerful Cast Member walked in, introduced herself, and it began.

We went through the history of the Disney Company — beginning, of course, with Walt himself. Then we went over other aspects of the company: what it owns, its goals and values, our part in making the magic. We were told to elect leaders in our small groups; I was chosen because I looked the most "professional" at our table — meaning I had my pen shoved behind my ear and no one else did. We played a few games, mostly Disney trivia, where small prizes were awarded.

Then, to our great relief, we got to stretch our legs with a tour of the Magic Kingdom. We roamed the Utilidor, checking out the cast cafeteria and costuming, among other highlights, and went on a scavenger hunt for examples of the Disney Basics: four principles (safety, courtesy, show, and efficiency) that Cast Members must always keep foremost in mind. After we finished our scavenger hunt, we returned to the bus and the rest of the seminar.

We arrived back home exhausted and exhilarated. Traditions really pumps up the Disney enthusiasm, and it also let me put to rest some of my fears about the program. Before leaving for CareerStart, I panicked that I would be one of the very, very few on the program because they loved Disney. I imagined everyone else was there less to work for Disney and more to take an extended vacation from school. And while this would prove true for many, it did not apply to the people sitting at my table, or to my other roommates.

Not long after Traditions, we received our Disney IDs, and we took a roommate trip to Magic Kingdom. (Jenni had never been there, other than the brief tour during Traditions.) Paige and Alex had already begun training, so they weren't able to go with us, but Jenni, Leah, and I hit the park, taking advantage of our first few empty days. We bought Mickey ears (for the entire group), rode the rides, and camped out on the sidewalk so we would have good seats for the parade.

I realized, waiting in line for some ride or another, that our group had really coalesced: we were our own little Fab Five. Jenni was Goofy; Leah, the princess, was Minnie; Paige, with her Disney knowledge, could be no one but the big mouse himself, Mickey; and Alex, with his quiet personality, was Pluto. Which left me, with a snarky little attitude and crabbiness in the mornings, as Donald.

It was perfect.

Chapter Eight

Amber Takes a Wrong Turn

MY FIRST DAYS AT Walt Disney World were hectic and slightly over-whelming — it was all that I thought it would be, and more.

My free time, however, wasn't exactly how I planned it. Your days are not filled with work (as much as I would eventually try to cram my schedule), and things that happen on your days off are just as entertaining as things that happen while on duty.

Take, for instance, a solo trip to the Orlando Target. Business casual attire was required for my first couple of days. I hadn't brought enough. I was scheduled to tour EPCOT the next day, and I needed a shirt to wear. I had already taken one trip to Target with Leah, so I was sure I'd be able to find Target, buy my shirt, and get back home quickly.

I set out around five in the evening. My GPS (which my parents insisted on buying for me, because I have zero sense of direction) was turned on, even though I didn't have the address of the Target store. I didn't have any addresses in Florida plugged into my GPS. If you have a sense of direction as poor as mine, I recommend that you put your apartment address in your GPS as soon as you know it.

I found the Target store easily enough, and within a relatively short period of time, I had a shirt — plus some more things that had looked appealing as I strolled the aisles. I checked out and started back to the apartment.

After about ten minutes, I began to suspect that I had never before seen my present surroundings. It was taking much longer to get back; soon, I started to panic, as I realized that I was utterly lost.

And I don't handle being lost well; I tend to freak out a little when I don't know where I am, or where I'm going.

So I was somewhere in Florida, driving in a random direction, and the sun was beginning to creep across the horizon, threatening to leave me lost and alone in the dark. Lovely.

I can't remember how long I drove. I had somehow made my way onto a fairly deserted highway — not sure how that happened — and eventually pulled over at a gas station. My phone, of course, was dead, and my GPS was also on its way out. I had sent a slightly panicked call to my sister, Hayley, before my phone died, and though I didn't know it, my parents were getting increasingly angry as time passed and I wasn't answering my phone. My thinking was to let my phone charge, then call my roommates and get the apartment address, and then charge my GPS so I could finally find my way home.

Everything was taking longer to charge than I had thought, so I ventured into a gas station to ask for directions to Disney World. I figured if I could at least make it to Disney, I would be able to find the apartment complexes. The guy informed me that I had missed the exit; I needed to turn around and get off at the Arby's sign.

I was now on an interstate, and I knew there was no way I would be able to find an Arby's sign from there. But it was better than nothing; at least I knew to turn around instead of continuing to travel in the wrong direction. Who knows where I would have ended up. I drove a bit down the interstate, saw an exit for Orlando, and took it.

I spent what felt like the next hour following signs to Orlando, and then signs to Disney World. My tension, finally, began to ease when I passed through the Disney entrance gates. I was still lost, but at least I was lost on Disney property.

But now it was completely dark. Lovely. I pulled over at the Hess gas station across from Downtown Disney and asked the people working there for directions to the apartment complexes. Just to suit the tone of the night, they had no idea what I was talking about.

So I continued to drive around the property. Eventually, exhausted and just wanting to be home, I pulled into Saratoga Springs and begged the security guard for directions, praying that she knew where to find Chatham.

I have never been so thankful to a Cast Member as when she told me emphatically that she knew exactly where it was. She even went a step further and wrote down the directions for me; a good idea, as I was so frazzled from my adventures that I doubt I would have remembered.

A few minutes later, I pulled into my parking space at Chatham.

A roommate cheering-up party ensued — not so different from most nights in our apartment, but it was much needed. Leah, Paige, and Jenni listened sympathetically to my horror story, and then there were brownies, jokes, and board games that made me forget, mostly, how freaked out I had been about being lost somewhere in Florida.

Over time, the favor was returned. One of us would have an awful day, and immediately the apartment would kick into overdrive, doing whatever we could think of to cheer one another up. Sometimes it would be as simple as clearing off the living room table and coloring (there was a lot of coloring in our apartment), sometimes it would be sitting around on the couch munching on lemon bars and telling funny stories, and other times it would simply be offering a receptive ear.

Chapter Nine

Amber Opens Her Electric Umbrella

EACH COLLEGE PROGRAM BUS has a letter to indicate where it goes: for example, the A bus goes to Magic Kingdom, the C bus to EPCOT, the J bus to Animal Kingdom, and so forth. In addition to a letter, each bus has a number (1-3) to denote its times of operation. Since these buses are available only for program participants, you need your housing ID to board. No exceptions. People often arrive late for work because they forgot their housing ID, and then had to fight with security to be let back into their apartment complex to get it.

The C (or EPCOT) bus is a cultural mish-mash. Chatty members of numerous cultures occupy groups of seats, leaning over the back or sitting in each other's laps as they talk loudly to one another. More reserved individuals, such as myself, are often found with headphones shoved in their ears, or a book in their laps (I tend to do both). For me, the C bus is the most interesting of the buses, and sometimes I prefer to people-watch instead of read.

My first ride on the C bus came a few days after Traditions. I had had quite a break between the frenzy of arriving and the beginning of work, and I was eager to find out what it was I'd be doing. The first day was our tour of the park where we had been assigned; another helpful part of the program for those who have never actually been to Disney World, or maybe didn't make it to all the parks. This is why we arrived at EPCOT early in the morning to meet in a random room tucked away in a random building. We were to be taught the specifics of our park, what it stood for, its history, the layout, and much, much more.

I imagine that for some people, this meeting is incredibly dull. I have to admit, there were times when I found my mind wandering to other things, especially since I come from a family that has a slight obsession with Disney, and so I knew a lot of the material we were going over. What kept our group from falling into a stupor was a group of French men, all of them tall, dark headed, and with a plethora of inside jokes (told mostly in French, of course). It seemed their mission was to see just how angry they could make our instructor. Whether it was comments muttered across the room in French or raucous laughter erupting from the back of the meeting room, not five minutes went by without someone receiving a glare from the poor woman trying to get through her spiel about EPCOT. Days like that, she must love her job.

After the seminar, we went on a tour of the park. Unfortunately, none of us had learned from previous experience, and weren't quite prepared for the chilly wind blowing off the lagoon. In my skirt and cardigan, I was certainly less than thrilled about taking a walking tour around EPCOT. We were there before World Showcase opened, and as we watched, a Segway tour winded its way through the pavilions. Our tour guide, taking pity on us (and I'm sure there was personal motive, too), decided to spare us the mile-long trek around the World Showcase. Instead, we boarded a Friendship boat, and the tour — consisting of a brief history and a few fun facts — was conducted from the lagoon.

When we got off the boat, shivering in the wind, someone in our group lent me his coat — a welcome display of chivalry that was hugely appreciated. We headed toward first aid, the most important location on the tour. It was there that the group of French students, quiet for the majority of the tour in the park, began to act up again. Her temper made short by the continual interruptions and the cold, our instructor abandoned her glares and walked over to the group of misbehaving students. Their protestations of not understanding her English because she spoke too quickly, at first blurted out interspersed by chuckles, were quickly shot down as she threatened to have them sent back to their complexes to delay their training. All we heard from the French students for the rest of the day were markedly quieter chuckles.

The majority of training is a blur to me now, for good reason. A lot of hours were spent in cold rooms in front of a computer, watching monotonous, energy-draining videos about the proper way to serve alcohol and what to do if we observed someone shoplifting (basically nothing, just take a few notes on their appearance and call security). Some of the training videos were specific to Quick Service, my assigned role, and others we had to watch regardless of our roles. There were more classroom seminars teaching us how to properly lift boxes and other mundane tasks. It was all necessary, of course, but that in no way made it interesting.

Eventually, I got to meet with my training coordinator. There were four of us who were being trained at the Electric Umbrella. I arrived at the cast building early and took a seat in the break room, where I settled down to read until the others started to show up. We introduced ourselves, made sure the shoes we'd bought were okay for working in the kitchen, and headed to Costuming. There we tried on our wonderful two-toned red shirts, baseball caps, and black polyester pants.

Disney sizes really do not make any sense; I'm not even sure how they came up with a system for it. I wore so many different sizes. Even within one size — 4/27, for example — they ranged from the legs needing to be rolled up to me having to hold my breath to fasten the waist. You can check out three shirts, pants, and aprons at a time, plus your hat and belt. I would usually gather my three from Costuming and take them all home so I could change before work, though later I just started keeping them in my locker at Casting and changed there. Once, though, I was down to my last pair of pants, and was running a little late for work. I showed up with my pants a good three inches above my ankles. After some mocking on the part of my manager, he sent me back to Costuming to grab a new pair — which had the same numbers on them, of course, but which actually fit.

After we had stored our costumes in our lockers, we headed to the

Electric Umbrella (fondly known as EU to those who work there) for the first time. We were given little slips of paper letting the cashier know that we were trainees, then gave our order and met our coordinator upstairs with our food. There we sat, ate our meal, and filled out forms on the service: Were the cashiers friendly? Did the fillers have a good attitude as they passed us our trays? Were the people in charge of cleaning up Beverage Island — the drink station — scowling as they mopped up another mess?

We were not wearing our name tags, but the guy bussing upstairs recognized us as trainees. When he saw that our training coordinator wasn't there, he ambled over to our table.

"You guys about to start training here?"

We all looked up at him. I, for one, was a little put off by the attitude of "Knowledgeable Cast Member" that this guy, Brian, was trying to give off.

"Yes."

"Do you wanna know how it really is?"

Now, let me just say, not all Cast Members are ideal. Not all of them fit the happy, upbeat, friendly mold that Disney requires. A major problem that I encountered was that a lot of people were here simply to get a semester off school to go party and score a nice boost to their résumé. After all, how hard could it be working at Disney World? Brian fit into this category of less-than-impressive Cast Members.

Of course, the other girls wanted to hear his insight into the workings of the company. As he rambled on about the inconveniences and ridiculous hours, I ate my burger and fries. When our coordinator rejoined us, the captivating busboy left to sullenly wipe down a table or two. Needless to say, he didn't rate very high on my evaluation sheet. Nor did he make it very far into his program, either.

The next day it was time to put on my costume and board the C bus, embarking on my first day of real work. Our training schedule had us arriving at noon and staying until after closing. We were assigned a trainer who taught us several new positions throughout the day and then showed us how to close an area.

Training is a tricky thing. I learn quickly and independently; I'm not afraid to ask stupid questions, as long as I know how to do something. Some people need more assurance or guidance, and others take it up quickly.

My first day of training didn't go well, so it was a good thing that I wasn't the dependent type. My trainer was an older woman who was supposed to teach me how to do the easier things at Electric Umbrella — bussing, lettuce and tomato (which means standing in front of the char broiler, Nieco, and putting lettuce and tomato on the hamburger buns as they came out the bottom), and filler, mainly. Simple tasks, but made a bit more complicated by the trainer's tendency to disappear.

I don't remember what position we started with — it may have been bussing or even filler — but eventually we made our way to lettuce and tomato. After showing me the basics, my trainer left for her lunch break, leaving me alone in the kitchen during a rush. I worked in silence for a long while, simply doing what she had told me. I asked questions when they switched me somewhere else. When the rush died down, I found myself working both in front of Nieco (taking pre-made but not frozen hamburgers off the tray and putting them on the buns) and doing lettuce and tomato.

The thing is, trainees aren't in the computer with regular Cast Members during their first four days. That means we don't show up when coordinators or leaders are moving people around, assigning breaks, and the like. They rely on trainers to ensure that we are taken care of. In my case, that first day I was forgotten. Eventually, someone realized that it was my first day, and told a manager I was missing a trainer. It turns out her break was almost over, so they sent me out to another position until she came back; then I went on my break.

Not all of my training days went like that. Most of my trainers were great; they made learning the different positions a lot of fun, and even cleaning the fryers wasn't as horrible as some people made it sound (everyone hated fryers).

Ovens was an adventure. I had an older man from Puerto Rico as a trainer, and he was also training another girl (a Columbian) at the same time. She and our trainer bonded over her modeling career and

Spanish fluency. More often than not, the trainer would show us how to do something, and then I would do it while the other trainee showed him modeling pictures she had on her phone. Which was fine, I suppose; ovens is a solo job, and at least I was going to know how to do it when the time came. It definitely didn't turn out to be one of my favorite positions; it involves a lot of lifting (boxes of frozen chicken nuggets, hamburger patties, and French fries; changing five-gallon soda boxes; taking all the leftover food down to the trash cans at the end of the night), and that's not exactly my forté.

The afternoon did provide some amusement, however, when we took the grease from Nieco down to the grease pit (not an actual hole in the ground but a big metal container with a hole in the front) at the end of the night. Not only did the area smell of tomatoes ripe from their time spent in the Florida sun, but the grease itself was not exactly the most pleasant of aromas. Having worked at the animal clinic for seven years, I was accustomed to bad smells, but my fellow trainee didn't possess quite so strong a stomach. While I ripped open the plastic, tomato-filled bags to pour them into the trash cans, or hefted the grease container (with my trainer's help), she was making trips back and forth to the bathroom. Eventually, she stopped trying to join us, and waited at the mouth of the tunnel for us to finish.

My fourth (and last) day of training was across the street at Fountain View, the ice cream shop. Its atmosphere was drastically different from that of EU; not only did less people work there (five people on average), but it was more laid back. My Fountain View trainer was wonderful — I didn't miss my break or anything! — and he taught me how to scoop ice cream, prepare sundaes and floats, and make waffle bowls (my favorite position). At the end of the night, he showed me how to clean the ice cream case — which I absolutely loathed, having to reach in and scrape ice cream from the far corners of the case — and then we headed over to EU to clock out.

I have always loved learning new things, and within the Electric Umbrella and Fountain View, there were myriad things to pick up on, from how to properly clean a trash can to how to make waffle bowls. In four days I hadn't learned everything I would need to make it through the next six months, but it was a good start.

Chapter Ten

Amber Bonds Over French Fries

"EXCUSE ME, BUT THESE French fries fell over."
   "Oh, no! Ah, I'm sorry! Here, let me fix them!"
   "Oh, it's fine! Thank you!"
Thus began a beautiful friendship.

Before I left home for Disney World, I had a momentary night of panic. I worried that everyone else had enrolled in the CareerStart and College Programs for the wrong reasons. I imagined they were all going to party, escape from school for a while, use Disney as an excuse to live in Florida for six months, and consumer as much alcohol as their bodies would permit.

   I saw potential friends in none of these groups. I'm the person who brings hefty books to a gathering, not the kind to get dressed up and go to a club.

   My fears were initially allayed when I met my roommates, wonderful girls who were there searching for their dream jobs. Our "parties" were trips to the parks for nice meals, ending the day with a game of *Scene It!* or some other board game.

   But just because three of the people I'd met so far didn't fit into the less-than-devoted Cast Member category didn't mean that everyone else wasn't there for exactly the reasons I feared.

   For about the first two months working at the Electric Umbrella, I was the quiet one. I didn't talk to many people, I worked hard, and then I went home. I chatted with only two of my trainers from the first week, and would try (and usually fail) to initiate conversation wherever I was stationed.

So I watched with a little jealousy as others who had been there longer communicated easily with one another, jesting and goofing off all day. But as much as I wanted to join the fun, I was too reserved. I don't go out of my way to initiate conversation; I'm bad at making small talk.

One day, working as a filler, I saw that a tray full of French fries had tipped over. As a filler (the person who puts the tray of food on the counter for the guest to pick up), you aren't allowed to touch the food. You have to get the attention of the person stationed at the window between the counter and the kitchen area, and they have to fix it for you.

For Cast Members still earning their ears, asking for help from someone at the window can be intimidating. Fillers would often grouse that the person "on window" (in charge of passing food from the kitchen area to the fillers) was being hateful or ignoring them. On several occasions, I remember standing uneasily — or impatiently, if I knew for certain I was being ignored — trying to get the attention of someone inside, to no avail. This illusion of hostility continues until you actually work on the line yourself. Not everyone inside is grouchy; they might not be able to hear you, or they might have a big order to fill. And occasionally, it's the filler at fault.

But that day, I still hadn't done much work inside (a privilege reserved for Cast Members who have been there a while), and it was lovely to hear someone cheerful on the other side of the window.

Beatriz, or "Betty" to her many friends, was the first real friend I made at the Electric Umbrella. With her energetic personality, her habit of switching from English to Spanish spoken so rapidly it was hard for most of us to understand, and her enthusiastic concern for the well-being of her friends, she was exactly the kind of person I needed to help me enter the social world of the Electric Umbrella.

Now, anytime I use the phrase "it's fine", she perks up and instantly begins to recount one of her favorite stories about the nice, quiet filler who she persuaded to go out one night with some of her other friends from work. When invited to do something with a group of people, my first instinct is to decline. Why, I don't know: maybe because

I'm just not used to being asked to do things with others and say no out of habit, maybe I'm afraid I'll be a killjoy. Whatever it is, I try to talk my way out of the offer. But when Betty asked if I would like to go out with a group of friends after work, I stopped myself before politely bowing out. Wasn't my goal to socialize, after all? And didn't that involve, oh, I don't know, actually making contact with human beings? So instead of backing out, I agreed to accompany Betty to the Ale House down the road from Vista. When I got there, I hopped up on one of the stools and took in the looks of slight disbelief. Betty's group had been together since January. They were surprised to see me there, and even more surprised that Betty had been able to convince the silent newbie to join them for dinner.

Chatting with people whom I hadn't known since the age of twelve was completely out of my comfort zone, but I did enjoy myself. Which came as a surprise even to me.

At one point during the night, one of my new friends happened to look down at my purse.

"Amber? Is that a book in your bag?"

I saw that my copy of *The Complete Works of Sherlock Holmes, Vol. I* was sticking out of the top of my purse. I probably made some quip about using it in self-defense, or in case the conversation got boring. Books act as a kind of safety blanket for me. I took *Great Expectations* to a sleep-over when I was eleven or twelve, threatened to bring the pocket edition of *Dracula* to the eighth-grade formal if my parents made me go, and brought *The Silmarillion* to my first year of band camp. To reach a level where I didn't need to grab a book on my way out the door would be a sort of miracle.

Leaving the Ale House that night, I felt odd satisfaction that I had managed to interact with others on a fairly normal level. I hadn't felt that I was intruding, or that I was unwanted company. And when I returned to work, I found that I was able to joke around with my co-workers instead of reprising my role as mute onlooker.

As I was the youngest person at the Electric Umbrella, Betty assumed a protective role. She looked out for me in almost every aspect: was I having fun? was I eating enough? was I working too hard? did I need another shift? Betty was on top of it all, and her mothering extended to nearly everyone in our EU family. On a day when I had forgotten to bring my lunch, I stopped by the break room downstairs to shed my ball cap and red shirt (it's against the rules to make any kind of purchase in your costume), and went out front to buy some food. Betty was working register, so naturally I headed to her register so we could chat while I paid for my food. As soon as she saw me, her face changed.

"You cannot buy anything today, flakita!" ["Flakita" means skinny.]

"But, Betty, I forgot my lunch! I need to eat something!"

"Ah," she replied, eyebrows raised, "but your mami knew you would forget. Go and look in my cooler; I made lunches for you and Em (another co-worker). Yours is the one with meat on it. Put it in the microwave for forty seconds, until the cheese melts."

Several other occasions called for Betty's intervention as well.

Once I had started hanging out with people from work, we went regularly to the usual Cast Member haunts: Steak 'n Shake, IHOP on International Waffle Day (I don't think anyone ordered the waffles, though), and especially Buffalo Wild Wings on Wednesday nights for karaoke. For me, with so little social experience, Buffalo Wild Wings was the closest thing to a club I'd ever seen. Too many bodies pressed in a little space, both inside the restaurant and out, with music pulsing so loudly you had to shout in someone's ear to be heard. But karaoke night was always a treat, since it drew such a diverse crowd: people there on dares, people who'd had too much alcohol, groups of girls who giggled more than sang, and lots of others. My particular favorite was a couple of cowboys—boots, hats, plaid, and all—who started out the night rapping but got progressively more country with each passing hour. Betty insisted on taking photos with them once the lights came on.

Many nights we stayed until closing time. Then our group would usually cross the street to McDonalds for a snack before we were ready to drive home. On one such night, as we milled about outside the club, waiting for everyone to find one another, I was talking with Emily (a co-worker at Electric Umbrella) when a guy came up and asked me a few questions. Not wanting to appear rude, I answered his questions and then did my best to ignore him. But he didn't go away. He and his friend lingered, occasionally commenting on my conversation with Emily. Naïve as I can be, I ended up chatting with him, until he made a comment in Spanish to his friend. Almost immediately, Betty's arm wrapped around mine and she pulled me away, explaining: "Mi amiga del alma, those eyes! Those eyes will get you in trouble!" I'm still not sure what kind of trouble, exactly, my eyes were going to get me into on that occasion, but it wasn't the last time Betty came around to rescue me from a dubious situation.

I'm sad that it took me so long to become comfortable with my co-workers, because they really were an amazing group. Sarah Mae, one of the girls from Australia, was singing a Kate Nash song in the kitchen one day. I commented on it, quite liking Kate Nash, and the next day she gave me a piece of paper covered — front and back — with the names of her favorite bands and two songs from each band that she thought I'd like. Rides were traded, days were spent in the park, and I became known as the girl who brought a book with her everywhere — including all social outings.

Being a Cast Member made it easier for me to initiate conversations with complete strangers. I had to do that all the time on the clock — chatting for thirty minutes with a guest who happened to be an English teacher; giving advice to a single mom who wanted to make the most of her days in Disney; or walking around with crayons and coloring pages, asking little kids if they would be interested in coming to the front and coloring with me when they finished their food — so the habit slowly leaked over to life off the clock. I would often go to the parks by myself, for example, to EPCOT for a cone of lemon gelato, or to Magic Kingdom to see PhilharMagic (my absolute favorite in that park), and would find myself in conversation with a fellow Cast Member who was in the park on their day off, or with a guest who had brought her children to Disney World for the first time.

For shy people (like me), the Disney College Program can do wonders. I'm not saying it will make you a crazy extrovert, bounding up to strangers and introducing yourself, but it will take away some of the anxiety that social situations can bring. Plus, it never hurts to make new friends.

Chapter Eleven

Amber Gets a New Gig

FROM THE MOMENT PAIGE came running up to me at check-in, we had gotten along well. Our senses of humor were similar, we were both slightly addicted to any and all things Disney, we both read, and we were huge, huge Harry Potter nerds. We also both listened to WDW Radio, an unofficial Disney podcast hosted by Lou Mongello. As any of Lou's followers on Facebook know, he occasionally holds meet-n-greets in the parks. Paige and I just so happened to have one of those mornings off, and so we hopped in Dinosaur (because the K bus to Animal Kingdom is a really long ride) and made our way to Animal Kingdom to find Lou.

Since we got there early, we wandered around DAK, as it's known to Cast Members, waiting for Lou to arrive. We stopped at the Yak and Yeti counter service for some Chinese food, then walked back to the Dawa Bar, where Lou would be holding his event. Already, quite a crowd had formed. Despite Lou's short stature, it was easy to locate him by the circle of fans pressing him from all sides. Paige and I grabbed a table a little removed from the group. We watched the African drummers performing nearby, and we pointed out the many Disney nerds who had been drawn to Lou's appearance in the park. It was refreshing to see people just as enthused as we were about wallowing in Disney trivia, reading personal accounts by Disney Imagineers, soaking up as much "back stage" knowledge as possible.

As we were sitting there, taking it all in, a man in a white Imagineer polo who had been eating at another table came up and introduced himself: "Hi, my name is Pete. What do you want to do for the company?"

Paige and I were a little taken aback by his abruptness, but it was an easy question, and we spared no time in answering.

"I want to be a tour guide for the Keys to the Kingdom," Paige told him firmly, explaining her fascination with the company and her love of trivia.

"I want to write," I said. "I don't necessarily know what I want to write, but I want to write. Something with Hyperion would be great, but I'm not in the least picky."

We stood around chatting a bit more about our goals for the future, and soon the crowds had dwindled. Pete led us over to the table where Lou had set his bags and introduced us, telling Lou that Paige wanted to be a tour guide. Lou whipped out copies of some of his audio tours, and while Paige went into another telling of her love of all things Disney, I was led over to a man I had never seen before.

"Hey, Tim. This is Amber. Amber, this is Tim Foster, one of the co-editors of *Celebrations* magazine. Tim, this girl wants to be a writer."

I felt three steps behind as I struggled to keep up with what was happening. Tim, with a look of excitement, took hold of my arm and walked me to a secluded area a few feet away.

"So you want to write? What do you want to write about? Have you read *Celebrations* before?"

I stared at him bemusedly for a moment. It was almost as if the words were taking too long to register with my brain. " What do I want to write?" I repeated aloud. "Um … well, anything, really. I love Disney, and I love writing. Any combination of the two is something I would be interested in. And no, actually, I have never heard of *Celebrations*."

As soon as I said it, I wondered if that was a smart thing to do, admitting to the co-editor that I had never heard of his magazine.

"What about the parks?" Tim asked. "Anything in particular you want to write about the parks?"

I continued to lag a couple of seconds behind in the conversation. "Well," I said hesitantly, "EPCOT is my favorite park, and the World Showcase is my favorite thing about EPCOT. I could spend an entire week there and not feel the urge to go to another park."

"Good! Good! I have been thinking for a while about doing a special edition covering all the World Showcase pavilions; I'm glad to hear others would be interested in it. I've got people covering some pavilions already, of course. Great Britain and France, for example, are covered, but there are plenty more ..."

And on he went, breathlessly ranting about which topics had potential and which had already been covered, or had been promised to someone else.

Ensured of my willingness and enthusiasm for Disney, but oddly deciding not to ask me to write about what I loved most, Tim mentioned that he wanted to do an article about Liberty Square. Magic Kingdom isn't my favorite park, and Liberty Square definitely is not a place where I had spent much time on past visits. But I wasn't going to refuse the chance to see my name in print, especially with Tim so eager to put it there. After I assured Tim that I would love the chance to write for him, he handed me his business card and we returned to the table, where Lou was signing the audio tour CDs for Paige, along with a few copies of *Celebrations*.

We sat around and talked for a while longer, the crowd now reduced to just a handful of people: me, Paige, Tim, Lou and his family, and Pete the Imagineer. Soon, though, Paige had to leave for work. The group stood and began to disperse. Since I had the day off, I wanted to head over to the *Finding Nemo* musical, which I hadn't seen in a while. Pete decided to go with me. Slightly confused, but at this point just going with whatever happened, we walked over to the theatre together. On the way, Pete showed me pictures of a wedding party he had DJ'ed at the Grand Floridian's Wedding Pavilion. Then, after the show, he gave me an impromptu backstage tour. By the time we were finished, Paige had gotten off work. She met us outside the gates, where the parking tram drops off guests. As she and I headed to Cast Member parking, thanking Pete once more for the contacts he had made for us that day, he stopped us and gave us his email. Finally, we parted. For the rest of the day, however, my imagination ran wild with the amazing opportunities that had come from our spontaneous decision to go meet Lou.

During my next day off, I camped out at the little white table just outside the Christmas store in Liberty Square. I had a new notebook in front of me, a new pen, and a bowl of watermelon. Rotating my wrist, sore from this sudden burst of writing, I looked up and took a minute to appreciate my situation: eighteen years old, sitting with a perfect view of Cinderella's Castle and Sleepy Hollow Refreshments, writing an article for a magazine about a subject that was more fun than any kind of work. My thoughts were interrupted when a mother hesitantly held her camera out to me, asking if I would take a photo of her family in the red sleigh next to my table. As this was the fourth or fifth such request I'd received in the couple of hours I'd been there, I smiled and assured her it was no trouble whatsoever.

Eventually, the park had to close — early, as luck would have it, since it was grad night — and I drove back home to type up what I had written. I spent numerous hours researching and writing this one article. I discovered a plethora of facts that made the entire Liberty Square area more interesting, and spent quite a few lunch breaks at work surrounded by my notes and the excerpts I had copied from books in the Cast Member library. After a little more tweaking, I sent the article to Tim on April 29, 2010, fretting that my writing wouldn't be good enough for him.

All I could do then was wait. It was remarkably like waiting for my acceptance into the program; I pulled up my email at every chance, as soon as I was on break, or off work, or any time at home. Then, finally, I got a response from Tim:

> Well Amber, you've really thrown a monkey wrench into my day. Here I am, thinking I'm all done with the next issue, and along comes your article. I absolutely LOVE it!! So much so that I think it may become the cover story of the next issue (meaning I have a lot of scrambling to do!!). We're doing a lot of USA type of stuff in this issue with the Fourth of July nearing (American Adventure, the never-opened Disney's America park, Hall of Presidents, Main Street etc.), and I think this would be the perfect theme-setting article for the whole issue. What a way to start out, huh??
>
> I have a copy editor who will go through and clean it up grammatically, but basically I think this is outstanding. Some of

the facts are ones we've used already or are already in another article so I may trim them, but beyond that this is fantastic, thank you so much!!!

I would like to add you to the Contributors Section up front, do you have a nice pic of yourself (it can be casual, even an "at the park" one if you've got it)? It doesn't need to be overly huge but 600 pixels or wide would be great. And a short bio too!!

Great work my friend, hopefully it will be the first of many!!

Tim

I sat in silence and stared at this message for a few seconds, and then immediately ran over to Betty, who had just come downstairs to go to the restroom, and gave her an excited hug, shoving the phone in her face. She was almost as excited as I was, assuring me that this was the beginning of great things. She told me: "You will be a famous author, mi amiga del alma, and your mami will be so proud of you, because I knew it!" I called my parents to let them know, and when break was over, everyone upstairs in the kitchen was subjected to my excited chatter until closing.

Paige, too, had a certain degree of success with her dream job. To be a Keys to the Kingdom tour guide is a coveted position; people can work for the company for years before they are permitted to lead guests through the bowels of Magic Kingdom.

We had emailed Pete the day after our meeting to thank him again for introducing us to people who had potential power to influence our futures, and received a reply that he was happy to help. And would we be interested in going to Magic Kingdom one day to watch him play with Push, the talking trash can in Tomorrowland?

On our next mutual day off, Paige and I went to Magic Kingdom and followed Push as kids delighted in throwing things in and teenage boys attempted to find where the voice was coming from. After Push was done for the day, Pete took us backstage and directed Paige inside one of the buildings where she actually had a meeting with the man in charge of casting for the Keys to the Kingdom tour. Pete and I sat outside at one of the picnic tables. Shortly, Paige came out thrilled, clutching a script that Disney uses for the actual audition.

Paige and I hadn't really counted on any kind of networking while we were down there. Or at least it had never crossed our minds that, while out to meet a podcaster, we would have such luck in furthering our dream careers. I guess that's the thing with spontaneous decisions — you never really know where you'll end up.

Chapter Twelve

Amber Deals with Disney Stress

"OH, COME ON. I'LL be working for Disney. How hard can that be?"

This is an oft-repeated refrain from future College Programmers before they start work at Walt Disney World. They even maintain this illusion for their first few weeks. Eventually, though, the experience that comes with being a Cast Member strips away the mirage of ease and happiness. Just because the Cast Members you see walking around are smiling doesn't mean they're having a magical day. Keeping their temper under control is part of the job.

It's one of the many things you learn during the initial training process. Disney Cast Members must look approachable at all times: no slouching, no hands on hips, no pointing with just one finger. You are taught to be consciously aware of how you look to guests from all angles — at least, that's what you're taught. It doesn't mean everyone pays attention. And smiling: smiling is key. Smiling makes you approachable; if you look like you are having a good time, guests will respond more favorably to you.

It sounds a little preachy, and trust me, not everyone pays attention to these kinds of rules. You'll find Cast Members who put little effort into looking approachable. It's just not something that many people worry about, and something not a lot of managers enforce. I understand this attitude: it's often hard to tolerate the daily parade of screaming children smushing their French fries into the ground, and angry parents telling you they've been waiting for their food for thirty minutes when you have absolutely no hand in what's going on in the kitchen.

I really loved my job, however, and the Disney attitude made my work day better. If I could spend ten minutes chatting with a kid about seeing the orcas at Sea World, or asking a guest about their day, it made *my* day go by faster. Sometimes, however, even I had trouble maintaining a magical attitude, and on those days I just wanted to hide in the kitchen and never come out and deal with guests.

What some people overlook when they dream about working for Disney is the high standards Disney sets for all of its Cast Members. Being approachable is just one of them. Disney makes no exceptions just because you're having a bad day or don't feel like being social. If, by nature, you are *not* a happy, friendly, easy-going person, then working for Disney may not be the fun-filled experience you expect.

Paige and I had a habit of waking up a couple of hours before we had to leave for work. She would make us breakfast, I would make my coffee, and we would sit on the couch watching *Family Feud* before getting in the shower and then heading off to work. On one such morning, I'm not entirely sure how, I got my mental schedule screwed up. I was leaving the apartment at the exact time I was supposed to be clocking in at the Electric Umbrella. Stomach sinking because I loathe being late, I ran to my car and called EU to let them know I wouldn't be there on time. I don't even remember if I had my costume on, but I would be willing to bet that it was waiting in my locker at Cast Services.

I was a bundle of nerves. I don't take being late lightly, especially if it's for work. Waiting at the stop sign just before turning onto the highway outside Patterson, I glanced down at the clock to see exactly how late I was going to be. Out of the corner of my eye, I saw the car ahead of me ease up on the brakes, and I drove forward to follow them.

Except the people in front of me had just been edging forward, so instead of smoothly pulling onto International Drive, I ran Dinosaur into the back of their car.

As if the morning weren't already bad enough. I panicked — this was the first time I'd been in an automobile accident — and wondered what in the world I was supposed to do now. I saw the people in front of me get out of their car, so I did the same.

And they were speaking Spanish. Not only had I rear-ended some-one as I was running late to work, I couldn't understand a word they were saying. I knew only a few Spanish words that Betty had taught me at the Electric Umbrella, and I didn't think knowing the Spanish word for "bacon" was going to help me in this situation.

I called my father, already choking on tears of panic that were threatening to burst out and render me incomprehensible. He told me to just get their insurance information, and other than that, follow their lead; as long as there wasn't any damage to them or their vehicle, let them decide whether to file a police report. I hung up with him, and turned around to face the two men who were inspecting their car.

As I turned out, they also spoke English, and neither of them was hurt. Their car, too, was perfectly fine, though apparently the license plate had a dent in it. I tried to explain to them that I was hugely, hugely sorry, that I was running late for work and must not have been paying enough attention, and that whatever they wanted to do was fine. I was a horrid mess of rambling and tears. I'm sure I looked terrifying — and a little pathetic — in my Kim Possible outfit of a black tank top and worn cargo pants, with my mascara running.

I don't know whether I was making them nervous or they just wanted to get as far away from me as possible, but they tried to calm me down and we headed to our cars to write down insurance information. I called work yet again to tell them that I was going to be even later, because I had now rear-ended someone. The manager who answered the phone assured me there was absolutely no rush. When I hung up, the driver's friend was coming back to hand me their information, and the first thing he saw was that my busted ink pen had just squirted blue ink all over the card I was trying to write on, and all over my hand, too. That sent me into another little panic, because a blue hand is definitely not the Disney Look, so now not only was I running late for work, but Disney might decide not to put me on register duty because I had a freaking blue hand.

The guy lent me his pen so I could I finish copying down my information. When I looked up, the driver was also there, holding out his phone and telling me that his girlfriend (the owner of the car) wanted to speak with me.

She...was not a nice lady.

I realized that speaking with her wasn't going to get me anywhere, so I said nothing and tried to make sense of her torrent of profanity and threats. After a while, the girlfriend had expended her vocabulary, and apparently tired of listening to me breathe, told me to hand the phone back to her boyfriend. Which I did gladly.

At this point, a police officer pulled up to the corner and asked us to move our cars onto the shoulder. We complied, and he left saying that he would radio someone else in. This quickly brought all conversation to an end, as the men assured me there was no reason to have the police look over anything, because they were fine and the police would only charge me, and they didn't want that. With no further drama, they quickly got in their car and headed off. I did the same.

I showed up to work late, of course, but at least I had managed to stop crying pathetically. It was one of those times that I was grateful for the Disney guidelines, because I knew that it was part of my job to suck it up and pretend like nothing had happened. My resolve lasted as far as the kitchen, where one of my coordinators, Sharon, took one look at me and told me I needed a hug. Which of course made me upset all over again. So I spent the first bit of work around the computer, rehashing various vehicle accidents with my area manager.

The blue hand was cool, too. I stayed in the kitchen all day.

I wasn't the only one who had bad days, but for some people, their bad days started every time they clocked in. One of these people was the girl I had trained with on ovens, the future model who couldn't stand the smell of grease. Disney, it turned out, wasn't exactly what she had expected. Perhaps she had thought she would come to Orlando and spend her days coloring with the children, not lifting heavy boxes of fries and changing the sticky, five-gallon soda boxes. Within a couple of months, during which she had spent all of her time bussing because she couldn't keep up with kitchen work, she had quit. It wasn't that she was incapable of doing the work; she just hadn't thought the work expected of her would be so hard.

This happens often. It's not the number one reason people don't last, but I believe that some people look at things like the cleanliness of the parks and don't give a second thought to the work that goes into keeping them so clean. Even if you come to Florida knowing this is a real job, the workload and everything associated with maintaining the Disney name can be overwhelming. While on your program, it is likely that you will have bad days, even bad weeks. In our little apartment of four, there were days when one of us would slouch in, throw down our bag, and sag, defeated, into a chair. Cue the outpouring of sympathy and willingness to listen about that one hateful guest or the co-worker who enjoys making life difficult.

For a lot of people, working at Disney is their first time living away from their families, on their own, in a place they may or may not be familiar with. Buying your own groceries, managing your laundry to make sure you have enough clean socks, paying for gas, coordinating your schedule around bus departure times, and much more — it's a lot to deal with.

Even roommates can cause friction. Whether by lack of communication or by some little thing that tips you over the edge of a bad week, the apartment can become fraught with tension — which is why it is a marvelous idea to come up with some stress relievers while you are on your program. Make sure to bring some of your favorite CDs. Watch a favorite movie. Play a video game (*Lego Harry Potter* was very popular in our apartment), or spend a day off just lounging around in pajamas, toting around a Breyer's tub of mint chocolate chip, and watching movies.

We each developed our own ways of dealing with stress. I discovered the Basin store in Downtown Disney; their bath bombs became my go-to after a hard day of work. When my muscles ached from lifting and scooping, or from going to the gym just so I would be able to lift the soda boxes onto the top shelf without help, it was wonderful to fill the tub, put on some Michael Bublé, and read. Leah also enjoyed the delights of a relaxing bath, as her job at the Sum of All Thrills at Innoventions involved lots of heavy lifting, and Paige many times took her stresses out by blowing up aliens on her Xbox.

Leah and I also liked to dress up and go out. If things were stressful, and staying in the apartment was chafing at us, we would dress up, pick a park, and see what nice restaurant would let us wheedle a table for two. We didn't even have to do much while we were in the park; sitting down and having dinner, catching up on what was going on with each another, was enough of a detox that when we came home, music blaring and the sticky night air blowing in from the open car windows, we were perfectly content.

Several nights I went out by myself, just to watch a fireworks show or because I was craving some kind of sweet that would help me decompress.

It's important to take advantage of every opportunity to alleviate the inevitable stress. Your time with Disney is limited; why waste it in a bad mood? As soon as my program was over, I remember looking back on some of those wasted days and wondering: "Well, why didn't I just take a trip to the beach?" or even "Why didn't I just go to the gym and make myself too tired to worry anymore?"

Everyone relaxes in a different way. Know what works for you, what smooths out the wrinkle in your forehead and eases the tension from your shoulders. Something that lets you appreciate that, back home, others are studying for a calculus final or a Spanish oral exam.

As preachy as it sounds, it's something I wish someone had told me before I went down.

Chapter Thirteen

Amber Colors Eggs at Chatham

THE SERENITY THAT EXISTED at Chatham, 22301, despite the occasional hiccups of annoyance that inevitably bubbled to the surface, did not last as long as any of us had imagined. Our nights of laughter and Fab Five ventures came to an end around Easter.

Jenni was having a difficult time at work. All of us had had bad days, had come home griping about our job and hateful co-workers. Jenni was working an egg roll cart in Animal Kingdom, and homesickness was starting to set in. She had never fully unpacked. Paige and I knew that she wasn't having the best time; Leah, her roommate, and thus the one closest to her, was getting worried. Then one morning, as Paige and I were sitting on the couch, munching on toast and watching our customary *Family Feud*, we got a text from Leah telling us to go into the room she shared with Jenni.

Paige and I looked at each other after reading this rather cryptic message, but I think both of us had a fairly good idea what it meant. We put down our coffee mugs and pushed open the door. The room that had just yesterday contained mountains of clothes and half-packed boxes now contained an empty bed. Only Leah's things, on her side of the room, remained. Jenni's mother had driven from Texas to help her move back.

The entire Fab Five spent one last day together. We ate at EPCOT, and I remember all five of us sitting on the hot, sticky plastic seats behind the Yakatori House. There wasn't much to say. Jenni had already turned in her IDs and told her managers. She was leaving tomorrow.

That night we went to Downtown Disney, where Jenni's mother

treated us to ice cream at Ghirardelli, and we tried to grasp how all of this had happened so quickly.

Since Leah shared a room with Jenni, and they had the strongest bond, she was hit hardest. Paige and I were also upset, and when the time came to say goodbye, we all stood — some with tearful eyes, others with a look of sad resignation — and hugged, bumping against the bleachers of the outside stage as we swayed little.

In the apartment that night, we were still shell-shocked. Paige and I were expecting it, so our reaction was more a sad acceptance. Leah, though, was completely shaken.

By the time Jenni and her mother had reached the Florida state line the next morning, Jenni was ready to come back. If only she hadn't turned in her ID or given her notice, if only she had just taken a short trip home to visit her family, she might have made it through the program. If only.

A few months later, Jenni did make an attempt to come back. She found an apartment — or someone to stay with for a short while — and applied for some jobs at the local outlet. Her goal was to wait until she could apply for a job with Disney again; she wanted to get back on her feet.

She returned to Texas within a week. Paige and I didn't see her at all during her short stay.

When Jenni left, we weren't quite sure what would happen. Disney Housing only condensed apartments if half of the people were left — Housing would then either join the people in the apartment with the people in another apartment, or move them into a smaller apartment. Our questions were answered when, a couple of weeks later, we found a letter folded under our door, telling us to expect a new roommate. In preparation, we had to clean the apartment, and we also had to pick up new keys, since our locks were going to be changed.

A few days later, we met the newest addition to 22301: May, a sweet girl from Shanghai, who had lived on the bottom floor of our building with some other Chinese girls. She wanted to work on her English, and had decided that the best way to improve it was to live with native speakers.

Her arrival brought a mixture of emotions; Leah had just lost her perfect roommate, and we weren't sure how a new arrival would affect the homey atmosphere we had cultivated.

While it definitely wasn't the same as it had been with Jenni, things went well. May and I got along; she remarked upon my odd habits (such as wearing two different socks), we talked about our shared love of theatre and liberal arts, and I tried out my mediocre Mandarin that some of the girls at work were teaching me. I remember one night, soon after May had moved in, when I came home from a long day at work, showered, and grabbed my tub of mint chocolate chip ice cream and a spoon. As I took my seat on the sofa, May looked up at me, eyes wide.

"All for you?"

I looked down at my half-empty carton of ice cream, the spoon sticking out over the top like a flag of conquest. "Yup. All for me."

She shook her head slowly. "Wow."

May was working in EPCOT as well; International College Programmers (ICPs) who come for a year often change roles halfway through their program. May began working in merchandise at Plaza Towers in EPCOT. She enjoyed that job. After six months, however, Disney moved her to quick service at Sunshine Seasons. I'd often come home to find her slumped in a chair, dejected. Life in quick service was not poor May's favorite; she didn't get along with her managers, she was most frequently put on bussing (a plight with which I can totally sympathize, as I weaseled my way out of every bussing position I could), and, honestly, it's kind of cruel to make the change from merchandise to quick service. Merchandise and quick service have different atmospheres, and make different demands on Cast Members. It's likely that if you enjoy one, you won't be as fond of the other — that holds true for me, at least, and for May as well.

It was fun having May around. Many things were new to her, and it was entertaining to see how other cultures view America, or how some aspects of our culture are confusing.

There was, of course, some friction accompanying her move into the apartment: her habit of leaving her rice cooker in the sink to soak annoyed some of us, and her chopsticks were always in danger of going down the food processor. We all did things that annoyed one another, but more often than not, we had fun.

Shortly after May moved in, Leah and I decided that another outing was due. I believe this was our Brown Derby night; we put on our pretty dresses and got ready to leave. Somehow, as we stood in the kitchen before leaving, the subject of Easter came up while we were talking to May. She didn't know what it was, so Leah explained the basics to her: why it's celebrated, the Easter Bunny, coloring Easter eggs ... the whole thing.

May was incredibly excited by the entire concept.

"Easter tomorrow?"

"Yes."

"So, the Easter Bunny come tonight?"

Leah looked at me, excitement glittering in her eyes. "Yes. He'll come tonight. Actually, when Amber and I come back, we'll color eggs for him!"

Paige had an egg coloring kit that she wasn't able to use (she had to be at work early in the morning), so we asked to borrow it. Then, after our dinner, Leah and I decided to assume the mantle of Easter Bunny.

We formulated our plan as we drove to Downtown Disney from Hollywood Studios. We would buy little gifts for everyone — Leah would get Paige's and mine, and I would get hers and May's — and then some candy to decorate with. An air of excitement filled Dino as we worked out what we would get. The bright lights of Downtown Disney drew us like moths, and soon we were out of the car and in the huge World of Disney shop.

Together we picked out an *Alice in Wonderland* tea set for Paige — who loved both breakfast and Alice — and some more typical Easter presents for May: a stuffed Thumper from *Bambi*, a large coffee mug with Thumper on it that we could set the stuffed animal in, and a large bag of jelly beans. Then we separated, agreeing on a rendezvous point after we had bought each other's presents; they were to be a surprise until the morning.

We had given each other only about thirty minutes to find the perfect gift, so — a little scatterbrained — I wandered through the

World of Disney before remembering a shirt (picturing an old cartoon with Mickey and Minnie Mouse in medieval attire) that I had seen a few weeks ago at Tren-D which reminded me of Leah, a huge Minnie fan. After I'd bought the shirt, I wandered into the crystal store, and found some little figurines of Snow White and Dopey — also favorites of Leah's. They quickly joined the t-shirt. With my bank account down to a few measly dollars, I retired the debit card and left to find Leah.

We met at the agreed-upon spot and, plastic bags rustling, rushed back to the car. We couldn't keep dopey grins off of our faces as we envisioned everyone waking up and seeing our "Nook of Celebration" (the useless extension of the living room that was supposed to be a balcony but never made it that far) decorated and full of presents.

When we arrived back at the apartment, May was awake and ready to color some eggs. We stashed our purchases behind the chair, and Leah set up the color and eggs while I showed May how, if you used a white crayon, you could write little messages on the eggs that would show up after you colored them. We made a special one for May's first Easter.

We colored our eggs — it must have been somewhere around one in the morning — and I have to say, it's one of my favorite Easter memories. May was so excited about the entire event that it was infectious. After we set the eggs up to dry, some of them glittering in the kitchen light, we moved to the floor in the living room. All four of us identified in some way with a Disney princess (even myself, the least likely Disney princess), and so we decided to color pictures for us to hang above our presents.

I colored Leah's picture — she was undoubtedly Snow White — while she colored my picture of Belle in her reading dress, book in hand. May took charge of Paige's picture of Jasmine, and Leah and I both teamed up to color May's favorite picture of Ariel. The poster-sized coloring pages took ages to color, especially as we were all the kind of hard-core artists who shaded in the sky and all the foliage, but we had some great conversation.

At one point, after we had been coloring in silence for a while, two sets of at least 96-count Crayola Crayons spilled out on the table so we could find our colors easier, May, dismayed by the desert landscape of Agrabah, cried out "So much brown!" which quickly became an inside joke for our little Easter escapade.

Eventually, everything was done.

We sent May to bed with the promise of the Easter Bunny's gift in the morning, and Leah and I hung the pictures and arranged the presents, jelly beans, and chocolate eggs in neat piles, shielding our presents from each other. Finally, around three in the morning, we took some final pictures, bade each other good night, and headed to our respective beds, excitement about the coming morning tempered by exhaustion.

We all woke up at the same time (except for Paige, who had had to leave much earlier), and it was wonderful to see May rush in, fall to her knees in front of her corner, and grab her Thumper. She looked at the stuffed rabbit, enraptured, and kissed it repeatedly.

"Oh, the Easter bunny came! So cute!"

Leah and I beamed at each other, then turned to inspect our own presents. She had gotten me a Peace, Love, and Mickey antenna topper; a Donald Duck keychain; and a notepad decorated with Belle's yellow ball gown. And, the massive part, a gift basket from Basin, containing some of my favorite bath bombs, bath salts, and more.

After talking about our presents for a few minutes, we all crawled back in our beds to wait for our alarms to go off once more, this time waking us for work.

When Leah met me in the kitchen later, she told me, another large smile on her face, "May fell asleep curled up with the little Thumper. It was fun being the Easter Bunny!"

Chapter Fourteen

Amber Learns Where Things Go

I LOOKED BEHIND ME on the bus, searching for the girl who had passed me wearing a straw hat.

"Hey, do you work at the Sunset Ranch?"

"Yeah, why?"

"Oh, I'm deployed, and was wondering where I go to get everything."

Something that made me and some of my friends anxious during our first few days at Disney World, and then again when we were deployed (temporarily assigned to a new work location), was where to find what we needed. Where would we put our bags? Where did we pick up costumes? Did we have to bring our own lunch to work, or was there something like a cafeteria or a restaurant for Cast Members?

For your workplace, obviously, you'll receive training. As part of orientation, you'll take a tour of the Cast Member building in the park where you'll be working. Each park has its own Cast Member building (or Utilidor, in the case of Magic Kingdom), and if you ride the Disney bus to work from your apartment, that's where it will drop you off, with the exception of Animal Kingdom.

Once you're inside, Cast Members are happy to point you toward costuming or bathroom/changing rooms. I was a little overwhelmed at first, but everything is set up so well that it's easy to navigate.

There are security guards at the entrance to these buildings who'll check your ID and bag before they let you enter. One security guard, Tom, was usually on duty when I left EPCOT for the night, and he was one of the happiest guys there. Every night, I would say goodnight to him on the way out, and he would answer likewise.

One night I had changed out of my work shirt before heading toward the exit. I was pleasantly surprised when Tom remembered my name, even without a nametag. He must see hundreds of Cast Members every night, and yet he remembered my name; it goes to show that the magic doesn't happen only onstage. The Cast Members backstage are just as special, even if they don't always get the appreciation those on stage receive.

I had my picture taken with Tom during one of my last nights in the park.

For meals, Cast Members often use the cafeterias set aside for them. The food is quite good, and I was a big fan of the grill area in EPCOT's cafeteria. You won't be shown the cast cafeteria during your orientation tour of the park, but any co-worker or leader will be happy to give directions.

My leaders at Electric Umbrella always tried their best to be aware of who had brought their lunches and who needed to eat at the cafeteria. They wanted to make sure everyone made it to the cafeteria before it closed. When I was deployed, the leaders at my other position weren't quite so accommodating. Every workplace is different, however, and people with all sorts of personalities will be your leaders.

The more places I worked, the more I realized how different EU was; while I was there, we didn't use CDS (Cast Deployment System), the computer program that organizes who goes where, and when. It was easier not to use CDS at EU, because the leaders knew better than the computer who worked the different positions best. Someone who can't keep up with the back of Nieco can hold up the progress of the kitchen drastically — not exactly something you want to chance in the middle of the lunch rush. But since I've left, rumor has it that even EU has yielded to CDS.

Prices at the cast cafeterias (run by Aramark, not Disney) are what you would expect. Food at the grills and other stations range in price between $5.00-$9.00. Lots of snacks — bagels, muffins, candy bars, popsicles — are available, too. Aramark also brings in some chains, such as Subway.

Despite the good food and decent prices, many Cast Members, especially those in the CareerStart and College Programs, opt to bring their own lunches. I was a fan of making a huge batch of pasta and then portioning it in Tupperware. I learned that vegetables like spinach weren't great for reheating, and the ratatouille penne that I learned to make was definitely the most revolting leftover that I have ever eaten. But baked chicken with brown rice and some kind of vegetable like broccoli? The best! And really easy to cook the night before work and stick in the fridge, too.

Where you kept your lunch depended upon where you worked. At one of the locations where I was deployed, there was very little space, and the lovely girl that I had met and asked advice from on the bus warned me that it wasn't the safest place, either — despite the fact that it was right beside the managers' offices! I used a small fridge to keep my pasta cold, but I had to carry my iPod and cell phone in my pockets. Apparently, a few people had had their stuff stolen, so it was best not to leave anything to chance.

EU, however, had a much safer break room. You could store your bag in the manager's office — which is where I kept my stuff on my first few days — or, if you brought your own lock, there were small lockers in the tunnels just outside. I never went through the effort of doing either; our break room had some shelves, and I would just toss my bag on one of them, store my food in a fridge, and head out.

My co-workers at EU were really great people, and though they weren't the only ones who used that break room, I never heard of anybody having a problem with theft. That's not to say I'd leave my iPod or other valuable item lying in plain view, but I never felt wary about leaving my bag shoved behind someone else's stuff for the day.

If you're cautious about leaving your possessions in the open, you'll be assigned a locker in the Cast Services building when you get your first set of costumes, but the building can be a long walk from your work location.

My advice is to store your belongings in the manager's office on your first day, especially if you've brought stuff you'd like to use during break; however, if you're only bringing small items and a lunch box, you may not even have to worry about storage. I used the manager's office for the first week or so until I made friends with some people who assured me that it was more than safe to leave my bag in the break room.

Bringing your own food will save you money, but it's no big deal if you forget to make your lunch or dinner before you leave the apartment. Just make sure the nearest cast cafeteria will be open during your shift.

Of course, circumstances really depend on your work location, but rest assured, none of it is complicated, and Cast Members are always more than happy to help you out.

Chapter Fifteen

Amber Gets Deployed

IT'S RARE THAT YOU'LL go through an entire program without being deployed temporarily (usually for a week) to another location. Sometimes it'll be in the same park, but other times you'll have to learn a whole new set of directions and procedures. You'll pull up your schedule, and find that instead of your regular work location, you've got to report at some place you've never heard of.

Working at Electric Umbrella, I watched most of the CPs get deployed before it happened to me. They came back with mixed reviews; some people loved where they had been sent (usually because it had been a little slower-paced), and some loathed it. I was looking forward to my deployment with a tad bit of trepidation.

Toward the end of May, I had reluctantly agreed to fly back home to Tennessee to walk at my high school graduation. I didn't want to do it, but my mother insisted, and missing two days of work wasn't a terribly big deal. I tried to request the days off through the Hub, the Cast Member website where you can view your schedule, pay-stub, other jobs that are open, article databases, and myriad other resources, but my time-off requests were denied. I ended up going to one of my leaders, and after explaining why I needed the days off, he assured me that it wouldn't be a problem.

It just so happened that these days off were during the week of my deployment. I double-checked to make sure that everything was fine.

The girl I had seen on the bus wearing the Sunset Ranch costume showed me where to find my own costume in the Cast Member building. I picked out a lovely blue and white blouse and matching skirt, a subtle apron plastered with sunflowers, and, as they were out of straw bonnets, a white handkerchief that I had to tie around my head. I took my newly acquired costume to the changing room, where I struggled for a couple of minutes as to which way the bottoms actually went. They looked like a skirt, but were really shorts ... still, despite all the logic I put into donning my bottoms correctly, when I stuck my iPod and cell phone in the pockets, it was to find that I had still managed to put them on backwards.

It was a sign.

I always feel uncomfortable walking across stage in costume. One of the things emphasized in Traditions is Walt's belief in the show: people dressed in Western costumes for Frontierland, for example, should under no circumstances be seen walking through the pastel colors of Fantasyland or tropical Adventureland. Magic Kingdom is the main place where that rule is most noticeable when broken, and fittingly, it's also the only park where you can easily get from one land to another — via the Utilidor — without ever stepping foot onstage. I knew how to find Sunset Ranch, but I wasn't sure how to get there backstage (and it didn't help that backstage at Hollywood Studios consists of a bunch of bland buildings). I managed to find one little shortcut, but still ended up crossing much of the stage, my Gryffindor bag slung across my shoulders.

Fortunately, I had made sure to show up with plenty of extra time. I asked around and someone pointed out the trailer where I'd find the Cast Deployment System (CDS), and another building where I'd find a fridge and a spot to stow my bag. When it came time to clock in through the CDS, I did so, and was put out on bussing.

Bussing is not my favorite task. Probably my least favorite, actually. In the heat, with the lovely smell of the grease and trash located just off-stage permeating the air, and the oily smell of turkey legs wafting over from the stand ... wonderful experience. Throughout the day, I was sometimes sent to get trays ready for pizza or to scoop ice cream, but mostly, I wandered around wiping down tables and pushing the trash cart.

When another Cast Member finally told me it was time for my break, I was elated. I went inside to grab my stuff and asked where

I could find the cafeteria. Luckily, it wasn't far, and I made my way there, already missing my old job at Electric Umbrella.

I headed over to the microwaves to warm up the batch of pasta I had brought with me. What I hadn't brought was a fork. I wandered around to the food area, only to find it gated up, the container of utensils inconveniently out of reach. Already impatient for my shift to be over, I took my Tupperware container out of the microwave and found an isolated seat in the sparsely-populated dining area. Eating pasta with my fingers was a pleasant way to break up the frustrating day. One of the guys from the Facebook group who I'd met during check-in drifted over to where I was sitting, and we chatted for a bit, he complimenting me on my lovely white handkerchief and glowing air of positivity. Far too soon, my break was over, and I made my way past the dumpsters to the CDS trailer, ready to clock in and receive my closing assignment. Bussing, of course.

Thankfully, a few other CPs were also bussing, and as the area filtered out after Fantasmic, it was nice to chat with them; I had spent most of the day in silence. I watched in exasperated amusement as a guest hopped up on one of the tables and broke it; there's something funny about how people who have done something stupid always look hurriedly around to see whether anyone is watching them. I went and told a manager, who came out to see if he could fix it, then went back to sweeping up chips and scooting benches under tables.

When my shift ended, I walked to the bus stop with a few of the other girls from Sunset Ranch. We plopped down on the concrete, exhausted, and waited a good hour or so until the bus arrived to take me home.

The next day was no better. I clocked in, got a slip of paper with my assignment, and told the woman in the area I was supposed to take over that she could go back to the CDS for her assignment. Not ten minutes later, she had returned, grabbing hold of my arm and pulling me backstage. Not exactly in the best of moods, I dug my heels in and waited until she let go of me before I walked any farther. She refused to answer any of my questions as to why I was being dragged backstage, only to say that the leader wanted to see me. Thoroughly bewildered at this woman's anger, and starting to get a little peeved myself, I walked into the trailer, only to have the manager ask if I had taken over for the Cast Member who had dragged me back. I replied that I had, and the leader dismissed me without any other comment.

I was put on scooping ice cream at some point in the day, which was probably my favorite position at Sunset Ranch. Unfortunately, I had hurt my wrist earlier at EU working on the fryers, and scooping ice cream all day wasn't making things any better. But making apple crumbles and sundaes was so much better than assembling burgers in a hot little building or filling up cups with Coke.

Needless to say, when the time came for me to pack up and head to the Orlando airport to fly back home for my high school graduation, I was thrilled. No more work at Sunset Ranch! During my short time there, I hadn't really spoken to anyone, and had scarcely seen a manager's face. There had been some people who were quite nice, but just as many who were not. Driving Dinosaur to the airport, on a fairly empty highway, in the still-dark hours of the morning, was a heavenly experience.

Back in Tennessee, I put on my cap and gown (and my Mickey Mouse graduation ears, which my principal wouldn't let me walk with), and sat for a couple of hours in the overheated gymnasium between two pregnant girls, zoning out during the valedictorian's speech and wondering who all these people were that I could have sworn I'd never seen. I walked across the stage, chatted with the few fellow graduates who I knew and liked, and said thank you to the family members who had come to see me.

I was back in Florida in no time. I walked in to my apartment, threw down my bags, and hopped online. And saw a lovely message from one of my managers, Eddie, telling me to not worry, but I should come in and talk to him as soon as possible.

Throwing a vexed look at my computer, I went back downstairs and drove to EPCOT, making my way to EU to find out what kind of trouble my leader had gotten me into. A few of the leaders I got along with spectacularly — TJ and Eddie, in particular — because we were smart-asses, and we could get away with insulting each other.

I walked into EU through the back entrance, and one of the leaders told me that Eddie was hiding behind the oven.

"What. What have you done?"

Eddie looked at me rather sheepishly. "Well, I may or may not have almost gotten you terminated. But it's fine now!" he assured me as my eyebrows shot even farther up. "Something didn't work out, and they didn't know you had those last two days off, so you had two no-call, no-shows. Three of them get you terminated. But they called us, and I got everything worked out. You don't even have the points on your record card anymore!"

I wasn't quite sure what to do with the knowledge that, had I taken another day off, I could have come back to find myself without a job, but since Eddie had already fixed everything, I left, shaking my head.

Deployment? Not exactly my favorite experience. I had never been so glad to have a shift at Electric Umbrella again.

Chapter Sixteen

Amber Recalls
Cast-off Cast Members

SOMETIMES THINGS HAPPEN THAT you don't plan for. Sometimes things go wrong, or reactions to an event aren't what you had envisioned.

For example, a lot of people arrive in Florida for Disney's CareerStart or College Programs with the mindset that nothing—nothing—is going to deter them from sticking it out. They are going to see it through to the end.

But then, of course, life happens.

While I worked at Walt Disney World on my first program, I saw many people leave before their time was up. Some caused trouble, did drugs, or got caught drunk at work.

One girl, who was absolutely a blast to hang out with and extremely amiable, once didn't come in for her next shift. When I asked around, I found out that she had been found the night before, passed out drunk in a bikini on the floor of the Grand Floridian Resort. And she was wearing her Disney ID, which only made the situation worse.

The guy who had trained me at Fountain View had a bad habit of coming in less than sober. He would recount to the other CPs how he had driven to Magic Kingdom rather tipsy, and would come back after a night in the park, only to realize that he had locked his keys in his car. On multiple occasions. Eventually, he didn't show up for work a couple of days in a row, and when later he reappeared, his

ion was rather bemused when he realized that he didn't have
b anymore.

And Brian, the CP who had been bussing upstairs on the first day
that I and a few other girls had come to Electric Umbrella? His wonderful personality couldn't counter his failure to understand that,
as we all had to sign in with unique user names when we operated
a register, Disney would easily be able to track money. He was terminated for stealing from the Mouse. I ran into him at the bus stop
the next day, as I was heading in to work, and saw that he had all of
his possessions piled around him.

"Hey, Brian," I said, keeping an eye out for the C bus.

"Hey, Amber." He looked self-consciously at his TV and his trash bags
full of belongings. "Yeah, I'm leaving. I'm totally just, you know, over
this place. I'm done with it." He explained how a family member was
on their way to pick him up, and we shifted our feet awkwardly, myself
fully aware of the real reason he was going. When the C bus finally
pulled up, I said a quick good-bye to Brian and headed in to work.

And then there are the people who leave and then wish they could
come back, like Jenni. Sometimes unforeseen circumstances arise
that make being somewhere else more important than working
for Disney.

Leah, for example, was the perfect Cast Member. She was cute and
bubbly — the ideal princess. She wore bows in her hair that coordi-
nated with her costume, she joked around with the kids, and even
when she was completely sore from lifting a 45-pound robot, she
could find something to smile about.

Around May, things started to get a little rocky. Leah was having
boy issues — her boyfriend back home wasn't being the best of beaus.
She was in the midst of planning a trip for him to come down and
visit. She had plans for every day, cool little excursions that he would
love. And then her father went into the hospital.

Leah's entire goal in coming to Florida had been to see if this was
what she wanted to do with her life; now that she was fairly certain
it wasn't, she didn't need all the stress that being in Florida placed
on her.

After his release from the hospital, Leah's father drove to the complex to help her load up all of her stuff to go home. Security, however, wouldn't let Leah or her father inside (they can be unaccommodating like that at times; though in this case she may have already turned in her Housing ID), so I packed all of Leah's belongings in my car and drove out to the front gates, then walked back to the apartment so I could get ready for work.

With a quick hug, Leah was gone.

With the disappearance of each roommate, Disney would change the locks and leave a letter on our counter informing us that a new roommate would be arriving soon.

The first key change I managed to catch, but the second time, after Leah had left, I drove to the apartment, ran up the stairs, and then realized that I hadn't had a chance to get the new key. I knocked, thinking that May did have the new key, but no one answered.

I slowly made the trek to the security booth at the front of the complex, hoping they'd be able to let me in. I was exhausted, I had worked an hour past the usual end of my shift because I had been delayed in cleaning the fryers, and I smelled like a revolting mixture of cooking oil and French fries.

When I arrived at the security booth, I saw May sitting on one of the benches. I gave a little whimper and sat down next to her. We would have to wait for Paige to come home.

After an hour and a half of waiting — I had called Paige, with no result, and had actually fallen asleep on the bench, my backwards baseball cap falling from my greasy hair to rest against slick shoes grainy with crumbs from chicken chunks — we heard Paige's sympathetic call, and I lethargically rose to accompany her and May to the apartment.

Jenni did go back for another CareerStart Program, working merchandise. She seemed to be doing much better on that go-round, and her new job was preferable to selling egg rolls from a stuffy cart. When I went to visit her in March, we spent one morning together in Magic Kingdom. Jenni was once again the vivacious girl bursting with the laughter I remembered from the beginning of our first program, not the lonely Jenni who had made the decision to pack up her stuff in the middle of the night. Her plan, she told me, was to extend, and then hopefully become a part-time Cast Member when her program was over. Unfortunately, her plans didn't pan out, and she left her second program early, too.

Two people that I chatted with on Facebook before arriving in Florida, Jake and Rebecca (yep, the girl I was supposed to room with), ended up getting together during the program. They're now sharing a wonderful, spacious apartment just a few minutes away from Disney World. They had been stuck for a little while in the jobs they held during the program, but both are now in different roles. They have an adorable kitten named Ohana, and last I heard, can see the Magic Kingdom fireworks from their bedroom window.

Leah isn't quite sure what she wants to do. Sometimes she was desperate about returning to Disney; other times, she talked about opening a cute little boutique back in her hometown. I'm simply hoping she finds something that makes her happy.

And the ones who got terminated? They never mentioned it much, and I don't speak with them anymore. But I'm sure they went back to the lives they led before they departed Florida, reflecting on their time here as a fun experience cut short before they were done partying.

Chapter 17

Amber Goes a-Wizarding

AS MUCH AS I enjoyed working, and despite how many hours as I was spending at Electric Umbrella, there was still plenty of time to hang out with co-workers outside of the break room and kitchen. While the phrase "going out" still gave me trepidation, I had slowly become acclimated to the social world, especially after my successful venture to the Ale House.

Buffalo Wild Wings was a favorite stop for CPs because it was one of the few places the CP buses went that served alcohol and played loud music. From Peerada, Jennifer, and MoMo, to Fan, Victoria, and Cristina, and even part-timers like Mike, Tenisha, and Stevenson, most of our group CP pictures were taken on the crowded floor of Buffalo Wild Wings. More were taken at the McDonalds just across the parking lot, though it wasn't the most popular restaurant for our group.

Restaurants open around the clock had a big advantage for us. After a late shift, we'd head out for a milkshake at Steak 'n Shake or a stack of pancakes from IHOP. I learned how to make worms out of crinkled straw paper. We waited at the drive-thru of McDonalds as Sarah Mae chatted with Mauricio, the guy with the headset. I stood up and got an award — Mostly Likely to Succeed — at our EU Cast party in the back room of IHOP. Others were awarded such titles as "King of Fryers" or "Queen Closer".

I didn't really go to the parks with co-workers. We spent so much time working in EPCOT that we weren't eager to head to the parks on our days off. During one of my last days on the program, Emily and I did spend the day in EPCOT, riding Spaceship Earth and buying massive Minnie Mouse bakery cookies. The parks were reserved for expeditions with my roommates, whether it was walking around the World Showcase with Danica; watching Wishes with Jenni, Leah, and Alex; or hunting for Lou Mongello in the Contemporary Resort with Paige.

Parties among CPs are not uncommon; there is always a party if you're in the mood to seek it out. I wasn't really in the partying sphere, and therefore only heard about the parties in Vista Way or at people's apartments outside of the complexes via co-workers, a number of whom were hung over on a couple of occasions as they labored over the fryers.

But group gatherings were something that I would attend, especially as I was comfortable in our little EU family circle. So when two of the people I worked with offered to have our CP group over to their apartment one night after work, I offered to drive those who lived in Chatham, while the people from Vista caught a ride with Betty.

Rachel, Sarah Mae, Yoshie, Betty, and I headed over to the apartment. Don and Morgan had arrived before us; Don had already begun the drinking. We were a little late — and by a little, I mean probably an hour or so; I had to wait for Betty to get ready, because I had to follow her there — and we all collapsed on the floor. There were half-finished card games, chatting, and I witnessed for the first time that unappealing game that is beer pong. I watched as the rest played a few games, poor Yoshie drinking Betty's cups since Betty was the one driving home.

At one point, Don got quite upset with me. He'd already had a lot to drink, and I had been given the task of distracting him from the game. I was doing a wonderful job, and eventually he got quite peeved and began yelling at me. I went to sit down while someone walked him outside to calm down. There had already been noise complaints from the neighbors, and a drunken screaming guy was not going to make anything better at three or so in the morning.

Our energy was pretty much sapped by this point, and by the time Don had cooled off enough to join us, we were all slumped around the apartment or lying on the floor. After chatting for a little while longer, we decided to leave. As Don lived in Chatham, I was given the distasteful task of driving him back, although I was quite honestly so vexed I would have paid someone else to drive him had I had any cash on me. But Betty already had a carful, so I agreed to meet her, Sarah Mae, Rachel, and Yoshie at Steak 'n Shake after I dropped Don off — there was no way in hell he was joining us.

I got in the car, pulled out behind Betty, and blasted my music so I wouldn't have to listen to Don talk. With the windows rolled down, you could still smell the alcohol roiling off of him, and at one point I had to pull over on the side of the interstate so he could throw up. Which just made everything better, especially as, directionally challenged as I am, I needed to stay in sight of Betty's car to know where I was going. By the time Don climbed sullenly back into the car, I had lost sight of her, but still somehow managed to make my way back to Chatham. Stony-faced, I unlocked the door outside of security, totally unwilling to even drive in and drop him off in front of his apartment. Without so much as a thank you, Don staggered out, and that was the last time I talked to Don for the rest of the program.

Paige and I, as roommates within an actual room, not just roommates sharing an entire apartment (and also the only two original members of 22301 to make it through the entire program), had the strongest connection. We had gone to meet Lou Mongello together that first time at the Dawa Bar, and we had taken Pete the Imagineer up on his offer to take us to Universal with his comp tickets. I had never been there, and spent the day riding roller coasters solo — Pete and Paige both got sick on roller coasters, and used up all of their tolerance on the first coaster we hit. We had lunch with the guy who did the voice of Donkey from the Shrek attraction, and I spent the entire ride in Dr. Seuss Land rotating in my seat, trying to keep the elusive Hogwarts castle in sight.

(Pete, a little unsettlingly, would call or text to see if I wanted to hang out afterwards; we found it odd that he never called Paige, and I was too wise to hang out with him on my own, Imagineer or not. He kept calling for a while, and Paige and I saw him a few more times, but that was all.)

As Paige and I were both tremendous Harry Potter fans, there was much talk of the series in our apartment. Paige had brought her Xbox — complete with *Lego Harry Potter: Years 1-4*. I would come in from work as late as eleven or twelve at night, toss my bag on my bed, and walk back into the living room, accepting the controller Paige held out as my little Ron avatar waited patiently (I never played as Harry). She would tell me about the cool prizes she had unlocked playing solo (our avatars would be wearing masks or brandishing carrot wands) as we tackled the levels together, playing for hours before conceding to exhaustion.

Around the second week of June, I had just printed out my schedule through the end of the following week. I was lounging around the apartment with Paige, and she mentioned something about the opening of Wizarding World of Harry Potter at Universal. I lamented for a minute or so about how I wished I could go — I hadn't asked for the day off, assuming that everyone else in Orlando would be trying to get the same day off. And then I froze mid-sentence. Without saying anything, I ran up to my bag and pulled my schedule out of whatever book I happened to be reading at the time.

"PAIGE! Paige! I've got it off! I've got the 18th off!"

Somehow, miraculously, the schedule gods had known that I had wanted to go to the grand opening of Wizarding World. One of the part-timers that worked at EU, Matt, had somehow managed to get in to Wizarding World early, and rhapsodized about it to me for hours once he realized that I was a fellow Harry Potter nerd. And somehow, somehow, I had gotten the day off.

Paige was just as excited. She didn't have to go in until six p.m., and immediately we began planning an expedition that might very well prove to be the best day of our entire program. We agreed that we wouldn't even touch our next paycheck, aware that we were going to spend obscene amounts of money at Universal.

June 18 dawned grossly early, and Paige and I were up and in the car before five. My playlist of Harry Potter soundtracks playing softly in the background, we chattered excitedly about what to expect. Around five, we pulled into the parking garage that was already starting to fill up. We made our way quickly to the front of the park, where they had already planned for a large line. We took our seats on the ground just beyond the Hard Rock Café, a fairly good position. And we waited.

After the sun had risen, and hundreds more had crowded in behind us, they slowly began to filter people into the park. Paige and I had both forgotten that we could have bought tickets ahead of time, so we lost our great spots as groups of people were let in behind us. We watched, anxious, as we stood in line to buy our tickets.

Finally, tickets clutched in our hands, we rushed into the park and began to catch up with the line. We hit a wall of people somewhere in the Jurassic Park area, and there we stayed for hours. I had started a new book (*Columbine*, by David Cullen; what every teenager brings to read while waiting to get into Wizarding World), and made quite a dent in it before we even shifted forward. Paige and I alternated between chatting and nodding off, or casting disparaging looks at the group behind us who had come outfitted in *Twilight* gear and could only converse by shouting.

Sometime around ten, we made it out of Jurassic Park. We heard fireworks go off, and cheering just around the bend, and listened excitedly as people nearby read updates off their phones.

Less than thirty minutes later, we were in.

It was a madhouse. Now, people like to warn me about going during peak times, and I just shake my head. Because nothing, nothing, could compare to being some of the first people into Wizarding World on the day of its grand opening. While I appreciated the effort to make the buildings feel as cozy and as English as they were in the movies, it didn't help to accommodate the hundreds of people who were trying to sandwich themselves near the shelves. The entire day was nothing but heat and lines. And more lines. And some pumpkin juice. While waiting in line. We made it onto the Forbidden Journey, the ride inside the castle, fairly quickly, and rode it multiple times. We bought wands and bags and banners and chocolate frogs. We waited four hours in line to make it into a clothing store, me nodding off, waking up only when Paige tapped me on the shoulder to scoot forward a foot. We had lunch in the Three Broomsticks (the framed picture of our first butterbeer mustaches accompanies me on every move), and pointed out the Extendable Ears hanging from the ceiling in Zonko's. Paige called in to work, telling them she wouldn't be coming in, taking the point rather than forcing both of us leave (I had driven, and she didn't have a way back, though I would have taken her). Fourteen hours we spent in Wizarding World, fourteen hot, sweaty, crowded hours having the time of our lives.

Of course, Paige and I did other activities besides indulging ourselves in Harry Potter infatuation. And it wasn't all fabulous; we got frustrated when one of us got in the shower the same time the other of us planned on it, and I'm sure that time she came home from a bad day at work to find some of her belongings upside down and myself secreted away in a fort in the living room, complete with brownies and a movie on my laptop, she was wishing for her own room. But really, we have little to complain about. There are some things you can't share without ending up liking each other, and toasting with mutual first mugs of butterbeer is one of them.

Chapter Eighteen

Amber Does the Cupid Shuffle

"HEY, AMBER, THIS IS Elchanan. You're going to train him tonight on Beverage Island."

Now, I don't honestly remember if Elchanan was the first person I trained. All I remember is that one day I walked in for my shift, clocked in, and a leader — Eddie or Patrick, someone — pointed out a new Cast Member with the "earning my ears" ribbon attached to the back of their nametag. And that's how I became a trainer.

This is the kind of thing that made the Electric Umbrella different from other locations — part of why I enjoyed it so much. And also part of why some of the people who still work there aren't such big fans. Electric Umbrella avoided the procedures that would have made becoming a trainer tedious, like having to take a qualifying series of classes (though the reason for the classes is understandable), much the same way it avoided using CDS to assign positions throughout the restaurant. I walked in, they told me to train some people on Beverage Island, and I did it.

I enjoyed being a trainer. Sometimes I felt awkward, giving orders to people often much older than myself, but it was a baseless anxiety, as most of the people I trained were fabulous. Luckily, EU is an easy place to train; my method was to show trainees how to do something once or twice, explaining as I went along, and let them have at it, helping out as needed. We would wander around the restaurant, me demonstrating how to bus tables or disassemble the hot chocolate machine at the end of the night for cleaning, and then letting them take over. We would chat while we worked, getting to know each other, them often asking questions about working at Electric Umbrella.

We would head downstairs for our break (I never forgot to take my trainees on break!), and I would walk with them over to the cafeteria if they didn't know where it was and needed food.

Being a trainer was an interesting position. It was a good way to further develop my socializing skills as I got to know the trainees, and to present myself as someone they could come to if they had any questions. I learned to recognize people's personalities, and how they learned best. Some people, like Michelle, preferred to learn things hands-on, asking questions only when they got stuck. I remember training her and Elchanan on Beverage Island, and she was right in there before I had even finished the demonstration, repeating things she'd already observed and asking a ton of questions. Beverage Island isn't a particularly difficult position — taking apart the hot chocolate machines to wash, melting ice, wiping down counters, and refilling soda lids and straws — but it can be a lot to remember.

Others, like Will, were … more interesting. Will had not been having a great day when I trained him on ovens, and I was a little uncomfortable throughout the entire evening, looking helplessly at Patrick, one of my leaders, as he tried to explain to Will that punching the top of a box of chunks to fit them into the freezer was not exactly in accordance with our Safe-D rules, whether he actually felt pain in his wrist or not.

My move to trainer heralded the approach of a new batch of CPs. The CareerStart Program is set up exactly like the Advantage College Programs — rather than staying the four months, as in a regular program, the Fall or Spring Advantage CPs lasted about six months. The beginning of May signaled the gradual loss of all the CPs who had been working at EU since I started. Marc, from Iowa State, who had kept us entertained with his wry sense of humor and eagerness to ensure the chunks were cooking well, went home. Ann, who was also part of our EU group, left us, too. Others, like Emily, Sam, and Betty, extended to stay at EU until August. Extending into another role was also an option; Don, for example, extended, but transferred to working attractions in Frontierland at Magic Kingdom. Sarah Mae and Rachel, our Australian friends, transferred a little later as part of their International Program; Sarah Mae moved to the other side of Future World, working merchandise in stores like the Art of Disney. Poor Rachel, who worked so much at EU that often she would sleep during her breaks rather than eat, was transferred to Dinoland in Animal Kingdom; working the carnival games out in the heat was definitely not a pleasant switch.

As sad as it was that our group had lost many of its original members, new CPs arrived. Kate, an ICP from Wales, joined us: she was definitely a character, and had such a habit of burning herself on every hot surface in the kitchen that eventually she was banned from working inside. Maud, a nice, soft-spoken girl from France, also joined us, as did Ian, from Canada, with whom I ended up discussing politics in the dish room on more than one occasion.

And then there was Mikael, one of the most fun, flamboyant people I ever trained at Electric Umbrella. His first day training on Beverage Island, he and I had an absolute blast; I don't remember getting along with anyone quite so well, so quickly. That night, as we finished shoving plastic utensils into the holders and refilling all the condiment pumps, I told him we were done and could head downstairs to fill out his paperwork for that day of training. Just then, one of our coordinators, Kerrie, came out, and told Mikael and I that we'd have to dump out all the knives and make sure they were put back facing in the same direction, a random requirement for closing I hadn't ever heard of. Kerrie's name can't be mentioned between us now without a knowing glance and the occasional stifled giggle.

Work wasn't the only place new people began appearing. After Leah had left, our apartment was again down to three people. Then one day, as I was sitting around the living room — eating, no doubt — I heard a shuffling at the door. When I opened it, I found myself face to face with our new roommate, Danica.

Canadian Danica was on a short program to serve as a lifeguard at the Disney water parks. She was extremely laid-back, and just here to have fun (not in the go-out-and-get-obscenely-drunk way, but in the intelligent, I-know-how-to-act-like-an-adult way). She and May got along very well; she and Paige not really so much. I don't think I ever fully understood the tension between them; it never caused much drama, but it was a change for 22301 — normally everyone in the apartment had gotten along effortlessly. This was the first time in our program two people just didn't get along.

I didn't really hang out with Danica outside of the apartment as much as I would have liked. Usually, by the time I came home, I was exhausted and not in the mood to go out. Danica and I did go to EPCOT, though, and had an impromptu dinner night. We decided to try the Coral Reef, where neither of us had been before. We managed to walk in and wait maybe ten minutes, and then we were seated at a table right next to the tank. It was quite an enjoyable night, and makes me wish that I had just gotten over being tired on a few more nights and gone out.

The end of the first group of CPs also brought on a slew of Housing programs. I had attended one of the Welcome Week parties, taking pictures with Goofy and Mickey in colorful Mardi Gras costumes and consuming a massive plate of southern food, watching men on stilts dance around the tent where the DJ was set up.

Toward the end of the regular-length College Program, Housing put on several other events.

The first such event our EU family attended was the spring formal, which had international travel as its theme. All the Electric Umbrella CPs scrambled to get the day — or at least the latter half of the day — off, and most of us did. The evening of the formal, I headed over to Betty's to meet up with all the others who lived in Vista Way. We lounged around Betty's bedroom as everyone got ready, fixing hair and adjusting dresses.

When it was time to leave, we piled into Ann's truck and headed to the convention center at Coronado Springs Resort. Walking in, we found ourselves greeted by a large group of CPs, widely dispersed over the enormous room. There were small tables set up with confetti on them, a dance floor and DJ, buffets, and little facades depicting several famous cities from around the world in front of which you could take pictures. We made our way to the food and fixed ourselves small plates. The Electric Umbrella CPs all managed to find one another: Vivian, Jennifer, Gemma, Don, Victoria, Peerada, Ann, Betty, MoMo, and I stood together, venturing briefly out onto the dance floor before deciding that we felt ridiculous. Soon, we dispersed, some of us sitting at a table, chatting and taking pictures with others who dropped by.

After a while, we got up, and Ann, Don, Betty, and I wandered around, Betty taking pictures at each of the city facades. And then we left, glad we had come, but feeling a little underwhelmed.

Every participant who makes it all the way through their program (or at least the vast majority of the way through it) is awarded Mickey ears, with a tassel stapled between the ears, and a certificate of completion. These, among other small keepsakes (everyone gets a large poster with the Castle and a number of sayings to remind you of your time in the program; I also got a purple plastic photo album) are passed out at graduation.

Our graduation ceremony took place at Mickey's Retreat, directly across from Chatham. I went with Betty and Emily. We walked over and picked up our Mickey ears, posters, and certificates first. By then, we were starving. Wending our way through a small building, we grabbed hoagies, apples, and sodas, then sat at the picnic tables and watched people queuing up to take pictures with the characters or dancing in the road — the Cupid shuffle was played at every housing event. Multiple times.

After finishing our lunch, we Cupid shuffled over to join the long line for pictures with Mickey and Minnie in their graduation robes, and then posed with Pluto and Goofy. Out of the lines, we found Donald and Chip and Dale wandering among the milling CPs — Donald was a must-have photo. At some point during the day, Don joined us. As this was after the drunken incident, I did my best to ignore his presence, and the four of us walked around with just a hint of awkwardness. We took pictures next to College Program graduation banners and played carnival games. Soon, though, Betty, Emily, and Don decided they were going to go to Cast Connections, a Cast Member discount store at Magic Kingdom, and I went to find Paige somewhere in the throng.

When I eventually found her, we spent a bit of time doing the Cupid shuffle with Donald and taking pictures next to the CareerStart banner, priding ourselves on being some of the few original program participants left. Pete was DJ'ing in Magic Kingdom that night, so we decided to drive over to the Transportation and Ticket Center and catch the ferry to the park. While on the ferry, wearing our graduation Mickey ears, and myself already starting to turn painfully red, the captain invited us into the cabin to take pictures. Once off the ferry, we walked over to Tomorrowland, where we quickly joined the back of the crowd in silly group dances, sometimes just standing aside to watch the smaller kids dance.

When the dance party took a break (Paige and I had been there for a couple of hours already; we were cool), Pete ran over and escorted us to the Astro Orbitor, giving instructions to the ride operator to let us view the fireworks from the top platform. Thrilled, Paige and I rode the elevator up and took pictures, sharing our view with just a few other guests — I would assume it was one of the least crowded spots from which to view Wishes that night.

When we had danced ourselves out, and were probably suffering from heat exposure and dehydration, we left Magic Kingdom and made our way home. Probably to play some *Lego Harry Potter*.

Chapter Nineteen

Amber Cries Her Farewells

"MIKAEL. IF YOU HUG Amber one more time, I swear I'm going to shove you into the cardboard compressor and push the button."

The end of my CareerStart Program came too soon — and yet in some ways, I had been ready to leave for at least a month.

After six months in Florida, it was finally the beginning of August, and I was preparing to make the immediate transition from living independently in Florida and working at Walt Disney World to transferring my green plastic bins to my dorm room at the University of Tennessee. The Travel Channel (my favorite) had been blocked by Disney's cable provider, and I was itching to start moving forward again.

Just because I was ready to regain some momentum in my life, however, did not make the idea of leaving Florida any easier.

When I got to Orlando, I had been terrified that I wouldn't be able to get along with anyone at Disney World — and now I couldn't imagine leaving the co-workers, roommates, and other Cast Members who had wormed their way into a place where not even the people with whom I had attended high school for three and a half years had managed to reach.

For the first time, I was faced with the concept of leaving people behind that I might never see again. I was upset about it. Australia, Canada, California, Texas ... my new friends were all about to depart to their respective homes around the world.

Rather than spend my last month packing up my things and getting ready to go, I spent every moment working or out with friends — late night runs to IHOP and Steak 'n Shake were common. Time was flying by, and as much fun as I was having, I watched plans that I had made with friends pass unfulfilled.

Paige and I, for example, had planned to return to Wizarding World, but never quite found the time to pick up our house banners to hang over our beds or have another butterbeer together.

We never made it to see La Nouba, and despite our best efforts, we never went up in Characters in Flight, the hot air balloon ride at Downtown Disney (we had tried on numerous occasions, even on Paige's birthday, but the weather conditions had never been right). I still had not gotten into a pool. I began to regret the days off I spent lounging inside the apartment, or nights when I was too tired to eke out the effort to leave.

But I was doing my best to make up for all of that.

During my last week at work, I was kind of a mess. Before moving to Florida, I was the person who never cried in public (Pixar movies don't count), whose possession of any emotions at all was debated by those outside my family. But my experience on the CareerStart Program had changed me, as corny as it sounds. I had grown attached to these people, much more than I would ever have believed possible. As goodbyes were being said during the final few days of work, I was constantly close to tears. The two married couples I worked with — Oscar and Digna, and Ben and Eva — caught me as I was going to the bathroom, and as they pulled their things out of their lockers, hugged me before they left.

"We just wanted to say that you are a good girl. We are very proud of you. One day, you will run this company; you will be CEO."

My eyes welled up a bit at their praise. As Eva patted my cheek, they disappeared through the door, and I made my way back into the restaurant.

When TJ gave Betty and me our evaluations on one of our last nights, I read his praise with stinging eyes. His entire goal throughout my program had been to make me cry (part of our sarcastic, playfully hateful friendship), and I only managed to make it through the office doors before Betty and I were both in tears.

The people leaving with me were equally emotional. Pictures were sneaked during lulls, heads were clustered in the lineup, and I developed a bad habit of wandering away from the back of Nieco to chat with Betty and Emily as they reminisced about our past six months together.

I said my goodbyes to the full- and part-timers who rotated through my last shifts. I hugged Tenisha goodbye, I acknowledged my impending departure to Sharon and Mrs. V, hugged Savitri (the most adorable woman) goodbye in Fountain View, and said a mockingly flippant farewell to Lanisha, the girl with the most attitude I've ever met; she started our acquaintance squirting me with a hose (which she denies, but I distinctly remember) and ended it confusing the entire kitchen by calling me Rose (as in Amber Rose, though I'm still not sure how she drew that correlation).

With a few days left, Eddie called me back from the register late at night to say goodbye, and while I managed not to cry while hugging him, Mikael swooped in with a hug — he had discovered that this simple act would totally reduce me to a blubbering state in no time.

"I hope you don't mind that, while I'm hugging you because you're sad, I'm also enjoying making you cry," he whispered gleefully.

I sniffled, laughing into his shoulder, and was promptly sent back out to the register. While we weren't exactly busy at that point, I did have to explain to a guest or two why I looked like a wreck.

On our last day at work, Emily and I managed not to shed a tear. We were closing together (I was scrubbing Nieco — my favorite! — and she had dish room), and though we were separated from Betty up in the hoods, we were glad that at least the three of us would share our last night at the Electric Umbrella.

As it turned out, the dish room was not the best place for Emily and me. It is perhaps the highest traffic area during closing, and people were constantly wandering in and out as we said our goodbyes. We joked around, me wearing my typical backwards hat and scraping blackened hamburger grease off the great metal pieces of the grill, and Emily spraying ketchup and tomatoes off the trays. We oscillated between shock that this was our last night and doing our best to ignore that depressing fact.

And then Micro came in.

Micro was a cheerful, middle-aged man who had come to work at the Electric Umbrella a few months after I got there, and I referred to him as my adopted uncle. He was never without a smile, and he had a habit of referring to me as the Energizer Bunny, a reference to how excited I got as I worked the anchor position. I hadn't seen much of him that day, but as he walked out of the dish room after our short conversation, he had mumbled, "It's just not gonna be any fun around here without you girls."

And that was it. I was done. My face quavered, and Emily and I just looked at each other, sharing that overwhelming feeling of sadness that this was our last night as part of the Electric Umbrella family.

That set the tone for our last few hours. Any time Micro came in — which was frequently — we would make eye contact, and I would start crying all over again. Several times I would just set down my sprayer and crouch above the chunks of hamburger on the wet floor, strangled laughter coming out distorted amidst the tears, acutely aware of how pathetic Emily and I — mostly me — must look. One of our coordinators, Jaz, came in, and Emily was reduced to the same state. It seemed as if our previous lack of ridiculous sadness was catching up with us all at once.

"Why are you crying?" Betty asked as she walked in at some point during the night. "Why? Que pasa?" Emily and I just exchanged glances and hiccups of laughter, not even attempting to articulate what was going on.

We stayed at work much longer than needed. When the entire kitchen was clean and emptied of people, we stood around and took pictures while posed in our favorite positions, like anchor or back of Nieco, and other completely random ones, like our closing sign covered with the names of everyone we'd worked with over the last six months. We finally ventured downstairs to say goodbye to our final closing leader and coordinator, Sharon, who gave Emily and I bouncy balls in exchange for our promise to stop crying.

My last night in Florida was spent in Ann's Vacation Club villa. A group of us got together, and I brought my program poster from graduation for everyone to sign. Betty made dinner, and we all sat around and chatted about our time together. I handed out letters that I had written to everyone, sitting on the floor of my apartment, telling them what kind of an impact they had made on me and how much I would miss them — which I refused to let them read in front of me.

At around three in the morning, though, Ann needed to get some sleep, and we slowly moved out into the parking lot, where we all once again started crying. This was it; it was our official last time seeing our family all together.

After much hugging and many false starts toward our cars, I finally got into mine with Mikael, Emily, and Mike, and headed home. I dropped Mike and Emily off at Mike's car, and Mikael and I went back to Chatham, where our buildings were directly across from each other — we could even wave from our bedroom windows. I only had time to change into my pajamas when there was a knock on my door, and in came Mikael, likewise clad, carrying his stuffed animal. I quickly ran into my bedroom, grabbed my Hogwarts Snuggie and stuffed Donald Duck that I'd bought just that morning when Emily and I went to spend our last day at a park, and within the hour we had both passed out on the couch in the living room.

All too soon, my alarm went off, and Mikael helped me move all of my crap (which really wasn't in any kind of order, or even completely packed) into Dinosaur, and after one last hug, went back to his apartment across the parking lot to sleep.

I wandered around the empty apartment in a kind of stupor. Paige and I hadn't spent as much time together during these last few days — her family had come down, and I spent a lot of time with my EU co-workers. Eventually, though, I had to say goodbye to her, and I wandered downstairs and into Dinosaur. My car was already stuffy from the Florida heat and the massive amounts of crap that Mikael and I had packed into it earlier. I put the key in the ignition. I was already late for breakfast with my parents at Boma. But as soon as I started the car, the finality of it all washed over me, and I only made it to the opposite side of the parking lot where, with shaking fingers, I texted Mikael to get his butt to the front door immediately.

I clambered out of my car and hopped across a little shrub, waiting in front of the door when Mikael opened it. He took one look at my face and hugged me.

"Aw, it just hit you, didn't it, dear?"

I chuckled a little through my sobs. I was still overwhelmed with the concept of actually having made friends, and now I was having to leave them (trust me, Grainger High School brought me nowhere close to any such sentiments). After a few minutes, one of Mikael's roommates came down to see what the commotion was, and Mikael reminded me that I had to leave to meet my parents. As much as I hated to, I knew that it was time to go. With a last sniffle and a hug, I got into my car and drove to Boma, stopping by the Clubhouse to drop off my ID and key.

I stayed awake for the entire ten, eleven hour drive home. I didn't want to stop to let my father take over for me, because while driving I didn't have to think about anything except driving. I played the radio loudly, rolled the windows down, and occasionally glanced over at the passenger seat, where Donald was sitting. But as purple clouds laced with lightning colored the sky ahead of us, Dad commandeered my car, and I spent a few hours curled up in the front seat of my mother's car.

An hour or so away from my parents' house, I took Dinosaur back. After a scant two hours of sleep, I was up again, transferring my stuff from my car to Dad's truck. By noon, I was moved into my college dorm, surrounded by pictures of my time in Florida, and already experiencing what one Facebook group calls Post-Disney Depression.

Part Two

My Second Semester at Walt Disney World

MY POST DISNEY DEPRESSION didn't last long. On the drive back from Disney World at the end of the CareerStart Program, I was thinking about two things: how much I had enjoyed the past several months, and how much I wanted to do them all over again.

It wouldn't be as easy as calling Disney, telling them I wanted to come back, and then driving down. Even though I was now an experienced Cast Member with positive reviews from my supervisors, I would have to apply to the Disney College Program just like everyone else.

Fortunately, the application process was the same—in fact, almost everything about the CareerStart and College Programs is the same—and I felt much more confident now that I knew what to expect.

Of course, they might still reject me. Disney does reject people who have participated in a program and then apply for a new semester. That didn't happen to me. But it was always a possibility.

Returning to Disney World as a "veteran" should have meant an uptick in my responsibilities and perhaps more interesting work assignments. Is that how Disney saw it?

Well, no.

And that was part of the reason why the College Program didn't quite work out the way I had expected. What I didn't completely realize then—but do realize now—was that I was returning to Disney World with my "guest blinders" off. Inevitably, the experience would be different—in some ways better, in other ways worse.

As I would soon find out...

Chapter 20

Amber Does Disney, Again

I BEGAN TO MISS Disney World before I had even left.

The long drive home, the drastic shift back to school life — all of it left me longing for the independence and fun that I had experienced in the Disney CareerStart Program.

I began talking immediately about returning for the College Program. Rather than discourage me from taking a semester off from school to return to Florida, my parents already began checking the calendar to see whether their next trip to Disney World would coincide with the start of the College Program in May.

During high school, I had taken enough classes through a local community college to build up a semester's worth of credits, so I wouldn't really be falling behind by returning to Disney. All I had to do was apply — and be accepted!

By the time applications rolled around, I was a little anxious about missing an entire semester of school. But I had good reasons: not only did I miss Disney, but the College Program would give me yet another internship for my resume, it would be another inch gained toward a possible Disney career, and I would be able to put aside some money for a future study abroad program.

But the thought of how many general education courses I could knock off if I stayed in college and gave up on Disney began to worry me a bit, though obviously not enough to prevent me from applying as soon as the application became available.

Sitting on my bed in my dorm, I waited for five o'clock with my laptop open. I had read on several discussion groups that 5:00 p.m. was the time when College Program applications usually became available. By the time six o'clock rolled around, I had filled out the application, passed the web-based interview, and had a phone interview scheduled in two days.

I didn't do nearly as much planning for this phone interview as I had done for my CareerStart phone interview. Rather, I scribbled down a few ideas — my top three roles and the top three areas where I would want to work within those roles — on an index card before locking myself in my boss' office at the animal clinic and waiting for the phone to ring.

When the phone rang, there was no mishap like last time. The interview went incredibly well. My interviewer was cheerful and friendly, and I felt totally at ease, slipping immediately into my Cast Member mindset — if I ever left it behind.

We chatted for a bit, both along the lines of the interview and on related tangents. I stressed that I wanted to stay busy — while I gave my top three roles as concierge, merchandise, and hospitality, I really just wanted a job that would keep me moving. We hung up, and I went back to work feeling very good about it.

A few hours later, when I walked out of the clinic, I saw that I had missed a call.

It was from the interviewer! She wanted to ask me another question, and said she would call back. Despite my moment of panic, wondering what in the world she could be calling about, I managed to fall asleep and her call woke me from a nap.

She had forgotten to ask what areas I wanted to work in. I gave her my list — hospitality, attractions, and merchandise — and hung up to begin my wait.

No matter how much confidence you have, the waiting is always miserable. Eventually, enough time passes that you start to rehash the interview, and pick out where you might have messed up. I waited for two and a half weeks, checking my e-mail constantly. My roommate warned me that the e-mail would come when I least expected it, but though that made sense, there was no way I was going to close my browser.

I wanted in.

I suffered through several false alarms before finally my acceptance e-mail arrived. I get e-mails from several Disney representatives, and so whenever I saw a capitalized "D", my stomach jumped a little. It was with great relief that I opened my e-mail with the purple banner, letting me know that I had made it — again!

I didn't exactly clear any of this with my university beforehand, an approach I don't recommend that you take with yours.

I have an incredibly stubborn streak, and I figured that the College Program clearly was such a good opportunity that they would be crazy not to let me participate. When I passed my first week of waiting, I called our Career Services, who handle similar programs, and got the number of a woman I needed to call if I were accepted. The meeting went well, and it was agreed that my program would be treated simply as a co-op: an internship for which I was merely pausing my formal education.

Everything — housing, financial aid, etc. — was put on hold until next semester. Other meetings, such as with my educational advisor, went just as well.

Packing started, but with less fervor than before. Being the typical poor college student, I wasn't able to stock up months in advance. My birthday in January brought toasters, silverware, dishwands, a small crock pot, and other assorted items that I would need.

I didn't put things in tubs until I moved back home from school. I had a two week interim before heading down to Florida, and those two weeks were filled with work, naps, and packing (which occurred much later than my mother would have liked). My parents and I were leaving on Saturday morning. That Friday, Mom and I ran around buying the last few items I needed, loading up my car (Dinosaur) and the truck my parents were driving, and dropping off my siblings at my aunt's house.

I spent my last night at home eating junk food and watching movies.

On Saturday morning, my mom graciously let me sleep in a bit before waking me to finish our to-do list. We dropped the dogs off at the clinic to board while we were gone, finished packing, and got ready to leave. I said good-bye to my cat, Lily, feeling like a horrible mother as I left her yet again, and then we hit the road.

The drive was better than it had been last year. We left at three in the morning last time, it was raining and cold the entire way down, and I even nodded off a bit as we passed through that final stretch of Georgia into Florida. But the weather was great this year, and eleven was a much preferable hour to head out on the road.

I spent the trip with the windows down, radio probably way too loud, and my stuffed Donald Duck (which I'd gotten on my last day in the parks during my CareerStart Program) sitting in the passenger seat propped up in the laundry basket containing my bubble-wrapped Harry Potter books. I didn't nod off this time, but I did clamber out of the car with a sunburn matching my father's: our left arms were a bright red, with a paler strip around our wrists from our watches. The sunblock I applied when we stopped for dinner did absolutely nothing.

We arrived at our resort, Port Orleans French Quarter, around 10:45 that night, and it wasn't long until I was asleep. We were awake early Sunday to hit EPCOT, and after Soarin' and a breakfast at Sunshine Seasons, we hit the World Showcase before making our way to Downtown Disney to finally ride Characters in Flight. After a nap at our resort, we headed back to EPCOT for a dinner at Via Napoli (it was brilliant; I highly recommend it).

Long before I left for Disney World, I met a girl (Lindsey) on Facebook and we decided to become roommates. A group of us had planned to meet the morning of check-in at 7:00 a.m., but my future roommate texted me with a change in plans: we were now meeting at 5:30 a.m. Despite having to awaken at such an ungodly hour, I couldn't help but be excited by the prospect of starting a new program.

It already feels completely different, though I couldn't tell you how. Maybe it's the confidence that I gained from CareerStart rubbing off on me; maybe it's that I still haven't quite recovered from finals week. Whatever it is, in a few hours I will be standing in line at Vista Way, probably chuntering under my breath about how obnoxious it is to be quite so loudly happy so early in the morning.

Chapter Twenty-One

Amber Goes Through
the Motions

"OR MAYBE ONE DAY you saw a kid drop his Mickey bar and went to get him another one, because that's how we roll here at Disney."

No one ever gave presenters props for having good jokes. Disney, with all of its pixie dust, is no exception. My senses — including sense of humor — deadened by a lack of sleep which not even massive amounts of coffee could revive, I sat through the plethora of meetings required of everyone during the first week of the College Program. Actually, I sat through them *again*, because they were the same programs that I had sat through during the first week of the CareerStart Program.

I began my week — I would say bright and early, but even the sun wasn't up yet — at four on Monday morning. I hadn't yet recuperated from my drive down, as my parents and I had hit the parks from the time we arrived until the night before check-in at Vista.

When I got the text from Lindsey, telling me that everyone (but me, apparently) had decided to gather for check-in at 5:30 a.m., I had been peeved, to say the least. But surprisingly, when I got to the security area, I found quite a few people already there. I had foregone coffee (a choice muddled by the early hours, I'm certain) and, after being smacked by the security gate because I wasn't paying attention, I saw my future roommates standing together in a little group by the fan. I joined them, but after the initial flurry of greetings, conversation deteriorated rapidly into silence.

At some point, the number of people in the security tent became too large, so Disney moved us across the lane, where we formed a spindly line two people abreast, the lucky ones (myself included) finding a seat on the ledge of a flower bed or on the railing. When the sun finally rose, some of us began to feel energized, and conversation picked up.

I looked through an enormous pin collection that one girl had brought with her; listened with sympathy as another told us how her old car had died right before moving down here, forcing her to scrap it and pay for a U-Haul trailer; and partook (with only some sarcasm) in the attempt at a Wave that petered out halfway through the line.

Finally, at eight o'clock, a wonderful woman on her Segway motored over and told us that we would start moving soon. She told those who had brought their luggage where to put it, gave family and friends directions to their gathering area, and warned people that running would not be tolerated, a rule that those who had been in line since three in the morning (questionable judgment) backed up with a few earnest threats.

The check-in process was fairly painless and took less than an hour and a half. We received our sticky name tags, filled out housing paperwork, selected our desired apartments and complexes, and received our keys. I had to borrow Lindsey's cardigan for the requisite property ID picture, as I had completely forgotten that tank tops don't fall within the Disney Look — I was just focused on staying cool in the heat.

After lamenting with the rest of my roommates over the extreme close-ups taken of our faces, I filled out my car registration paperwork (which required my ID, proof of insurance bearing my name, and car registration), and then we were on our way to the buses that would take us to Casting.

At about nine, we boarded the coach buses and listened to our narrator (who resembled Edna from *The Incredibles* and sounded like Flo from the Progressive Insurance commercials) give us valuable advice.

At the Casting building, we stood in line to receive our lovely stickers on our program guides that would tell us where we were working. As I heard "Magic Kingdom, you'll be joining us at Disney's

Magic Kingdom", I was feeling good about my chances. When it was my turn, and instead of "Magic Kingdom" I heard "Future World", I was disappointed, but the fact that I was back at Disney World helped buoy my spirits.

This process took about the same time as had check-in. We were fingerprinted for our background checks, received our pay cards, and were inspected to make sure we fit the Disney Look. After completing paperwork at a few other stations, I boarded another bus to take me back to Vista, where I got my car and drove to Chatham, my apartment complex.

After inspecting our three-bedroom apartment (which was much more spacious than I imagined), we all claimed rooms and began moving in. At some point my parents joined me, but left before three o'clock, when we had to attend the mandatory housing meeting. This meeting is dreadfully dull, and I think they choose to put on the most boring speaker first. That way they can work you into a stupor with their corny jokes that no one laughs at and the "instructional" videos filmed by actors worse than those on *The Bold and the Beautiful*, and hope that when the fun guy comes around for the second half of the meeting, you will be awake enough to go over the rules.

The rest of Monday afternoon registers as a haze of Disney goings-on, but at some point my parents came back to take me shoe shopping. Depending on how by-the-rules you are, this can be the most painful part of the process, especially as my parents decided to go to the Florida Mall, which is at the end of a road under construction.

It took ages to reach the mall, and afterward it took just as long to find a store that sold shoes that fit my parents' interpretation of the Disney Look. At one point, I was close to tears from a combination of exhaustion and frustration; any pair of black sneakers would work, as long as some other color didn't scream from the sides. Eventually, though, we found suitable shoes, and decided that my bag of leftover seafood pasta from Olive Garden would function just fine as groceries for the night.

On Tuesday, my parents came around to accompany me to Target, where I picked up things from a list I had started the previous day. I drove back to Chatham, and then later over to my parents' resort to join them for dinner at Beaches and Cream. We said our goodbyes, the promise of their return in two weeks making it a less-than-dramatic event.

Wednesday brought Traditions. I had managed to miss the early morning class, and instead boarded the bus at 12:45 p.m. with the rest of us lucky arrivals. I won't say much more about Traditions, except that even though I had gone through the same class before, watching some of the videos and hearing some of the letters read aloud gave me chills, and at some points my eyes and nose were a little itchy.

Thursday was my first day of work. I met my trainer and one other girl who was going to be trained with me in Future World, then picked up my costume and went over to my first work location. I learned that I'll be working at Image, the gift shop attached to Journey into Imagination with Figment gift shop; the nearby Captain EO cart; the Green Thumb Emporium outside Soarin'; and Seas (the Sea Base Alpha gift shop by Nemo & Friends). I spent the day just observing, and then spent the next day in a class to teach me how to work with merchandise.

Saturday was my first day of *real* work, and it began as one of the most frustrating days ever. By the time lunch break hit, I was ready to leave; I'd been there since 8:00 a.m., and had messed up on the register innumerable times. I printed the information on the wrong slips, gave guests the wrong copies, and forgot to staple things together.

The girl I was training with gave me some great advice: "These people wait in line for Soarin' for two hours. Waiting five minutes to make sure that their shipping information is correct is no big deal."

After that, I was a little less stressed out; it made sense, after all.

As I write, I'm exhausted. I'm sitting on my couch in the apartment, a mug of tea on the table beside me, listening to three of my room-mates chat about how much they like their jobs so far. Even though I'm a little grumpy from sleep deprivation and frustration, I'm ready to settle into my routine, and glad to be back home.

Chapter Twenty-Two

Amber Gives Guests Some Magic

I LOVE MY JOB.

That has been my constant refrain for the past week. Despite being tired most of the time (125 hours without a day off, anyone?), my work this year is far more energizing than the work I did last year at the Electric Umbrella. At the Umbrella, I loved being in the kitchen, interacting with my fellow Cast Members. I did not regret the lack of guest interaction while I was scooping French fries or putting trays through the dishwasher.

While I still miss EU, especially after I met up for dinner recently with some of the people who had worked there with me, I severely underestimated the fun of guest interaction.

Of course, there are the drunken guests, or the parents who don't seem to understand that to get a good picture of all the kids "flying" around the Castle with pixie dust, they should snap it at the beginning of the trip, when everyone has had enough sleep to be amiable. I have dealt with a few of the screaming children who did not want to take pictures, I have forgotten to push the "start over" button and screwed up at least two pictures for guests, and I neglected to give one family their receipt for package pickup.

As if that weren't enough, I also fell asleep waiting for the bus, and smacked my head into a shelf on Saturday. One of my trainers made me feel like an imbecile in front of guests.

But I love my job.

On Friday, I directed stroller traffic with another trainee. We wore silly hats (she wore a Viking hat, I put on an old school crown with red velvet and fur trim), used stunted lightsabers to point the way, and spoke in obnoxiously fake British accents. About ten guests stopped to take pictures with us that night; our trainer gave us Great Service Fanatic cards for being the only people she's ever trained who were asked by guests to pose for pictures. It was one of the most fun nights I have ever had at Disney World.

Earlier in the week, I trained on the glow cart, which was so much fun. I swear, when I'm working in merchandise I get paid to act like a little kid. I had a normal shift at Image, which was dreadful. We were understaffed, and I can never seem to do things correctly there. But when glow cart training came around, three of us (my trainer, myself, and another trainee) pulled out the cart and pushed it in front of the Land to start selling.

As soon as the cart came to a halt, I was in with the toys; I put the light-up tiara on, tried (and failed) to get my Michael Jackson glove to work, and began twirling a lightsaber. The best part? You get praised for doing that kind of thing! Sadly, none of the children who ventured over to the cart wanted to duel with me, but it was still immensely fun. I got to pin trade, give directions and recommendations, and chat up guests who were having the time of their lives.

It feels as if the beginning of the day is the longest. Depending on the work location, my first break will either sneak up on me, or I'll have a ghastly amount of time to watch the minutes tick by. I find it ironic how quickly times flies at my least favorite work location, but at Sea Base Alpha, where I have spent the last two days, everything moves at a glacial pace. But toward the end of the night, without fail, something ridiculously fun will happen that ensures a good mood for the end of the shift.

Sunday, for instance, was incredibly slow. I was working at Sea Base, and while I was having a blast, the day was dragging by. Only three people typically work there; we had time to stock everything, straighten the plush as soon as it was messed up, and I spent an absurd amount of time playing with the bubble gun. (Have I mentioned that I get paid to act like a little kid?)

When I felt like an hour had passed, I would look at the register to realize only a quarter of that time had gone by. I made innumerable runs to the stock room, swept up spilled sugar powder, and chatted with as many guests as I could.

Near the close of my shift, I found a poor Crush doll that had lost its voice. A little delirious from exhaustion, I decided to give Crush a pink Mickey head bracelet, strap on a Disney Conservation button (because Crush wants everyone to donate to help save his fellow marine life), and sit him on my shoulder with one of his fins looped around my neck.

Eventually, other accoutrements were added (including a shark tooth necklace, because Crush eats sharks for breakfast, dude), and I quite enjoyed the strange looks I got from children and adults alike as I ran around for an hour with a twelve-inch turtle perched on my shoulder.

Fifteen minutes before my shift ended, a family of four walked in, and I started talking with the two little girls. Both of them were overjoyed at the fact that they were in Disney, and the youngest was practically bouncing off the walls with excitement. I knelt on the floor and started talking turtle with them (as in 'dude' and 'wicked', often!), and we went over everything: where they were staying, how long, what their favorite color was, what they were most looking forward to, what their favorite movies were…

For at least ten minutes I sat there and talked with these girls, and when it came time for them to leave, their father came up and shook my hand, thanking me for managing to keep his girls entertained while he and his wife had a conversation with another Cast Member. As they left, and I got ready to do the same, they promised to come look for me later this week, when they go ride Figment (the eldest's favorite ride).

I feel, at this point, as if I have been down here for ages, rather than about to embark on my third week. Although I'm still waiting for certain aspects of my routine to establish themselves, I'm fairly confident about my work, and have felt at home in my apartment since the second or third night.

I can already see the drastic difference between my two roles (last time it was quick service), and while I can't determine which is my favorite, I can definitely say that I believe my experience this year will turn out to be just as phenomenal as it was last year.

Chapter Twenty-Three

Amber Keels Over

THE THEME OF THE past week has been chaos, with very little relief.

Not all of it has been bad chaos, exactly, but it has been about three weeks since I moved in, and I still have puffy bags under my eyes at all hours of the day.

Monday began on a poor note. It wasn't a bad shift — eight hours, mid-day — and I was sent out to work the squeeze breeze cart in front of the Land. My coordinator helped me maneuver the unwieldy cart into the shade, and I was given an apron (but no calculator, which presages disaster for an English major!) with some seed cash for making change.

I had fun for a bit. I was in the direct path of the guests booking it to Soarin' before all the FastPasses had been distributed and the line not worth a second look, so I was able to interact with quite a few of them. One man doubled back to shake my hand and loudly applaud that I was the first Cast Member he'd met on his trip to speak to him for no reason other than pleasantness.

I had been out on the water cart for maybe an hour when I began to regret having left my own water bottle at the apartment. It was on the floor where I'd kicked it while getting ready for work that morning. I felt a little faint, but thought it was simply from thinking too much about the heat.

I met several families who were having a marvelous time, and obligingly sprayed several guests with the wonderful (and expensive) misting fans. My good humor fled, just a bit, when a large group came up and asked to purchase twenty bottles of water. Twenty.

As soon as I heard the number — a double-digit number! — my brain, programmed as it is for semantics not mathematics, promptly went into panic mode and shut down.

I could all but hear the little sirens warning me that I would not be able to multiply $2.50 by 20. I stared stupidly at the guests. It was no relief when they reduced their order to eight bottles. I looked pleadingly at a couple of nearby Cast Members who were escorting guests on a tour of the park, and one of them said: "Well, two bottles of water equals five dollars", which should have helped me figure out the cost, but in my state it did nothing but frustrate me further.

Finally, we figured it out, and as I arranged the remaining water bottles in my cart to fill in the gaps, the simplicity of the math finally struck me, and I was glad that I had decided not to major in business, after all.

Shortly after the water people left, I began to feel as if I were going to pass out.

Working at an animal clinic for years has made me intimately acquainted with oncoming unconsciousness. I began to feel cold and noticed that my fingers had gone pale. I looked around pleadingly for my relief to emerge from the crowd. I had been on the cart for a while, and was sure someone would be coming soon to relieve me.

When no one came, despite my telepathic pleas, I called over to the Cast Member standing under an umbrella a few yards away. She made her way over, and I asked if it was okay if I sat down while she radioed for someone from Image to come take my place. Halfway through my sentence, I changed the query to a fact, and knelt in the shadow of my cart.

The difference between having male Leaders and female Leaders was striking.

When I had almost passed out at the Electric Umbrella last year, my male Leader belatedly (it took over ten minutes to find him) authorized me to move into the air conditioning and gave me a cookie.

This time, two female Leaders came right over, one of them literally taking me by the arm and leading me to our break room, where she made me sit and drink water while she microwaved the lunch I had brought. I was given more food to eat than I could have possibly imagined ingesting, and the Leaders stopped by regularly to make sure I was, in fact, eating it all. For the rest of the day, our coordinator walked me to and from the computer for my assignments, making sure I wasn't put back outside.

I haven't forgotten my water bottle since.

The rest of the week passed uneventfully.

On Thursday, I finally had a day off. I spent it at the park with some of my roommates, enjoying myself as a guest instead of having to act the part of a Cast Member. I didn't mind in the least that we went to EPCOT, because it is, after all, my favorite park. Working in Future World has only lessened that area's appeal, which was never great in the first place. The World Showcase remains my favorite of all the areas in Disney World.

On Friday, I ventured out with people from work. Last year, during CareerStart, it took a good two months before I warmed up to anyone. Since then, I've improved my socialization skills, and I was invited to play in Hollywood Studios after work — not by anyone in my location, but by two people in Attractions who share our break room and with whom I had become friendly.

When one of them mentioned that I would finally get to ride Star Tours, I couldn't refuse. I was glad that I had chosen (grudgingly, at first) to join him, because we managed to hit Rock 'n' Roller coaster and Star Tours twice, Tower of Terror once, and see Fantasmic; I consider all of this a great accomplishment, and a wonderful way to spend my free time.

On Saturday, my family arrived for their first visit of my program, and that night I met up with them and my brothers (but not my sister, who had other plans). I returned home tired and only slightly ready for work the next morning.

I awoke early, got my myself ready, had some coffee, and went to work. I clocked in for my 11:00 a.m. to 8:00 p.m. shift at Image, got my assignment... and then a coordinator walked over and said I was in the wrong location — and thirty minutes late!

I stared at her, dumbfounded. Had I not just checked my schedule, which had me down for an 11-8 shift? I spoke with strong conviction that she must be wrong, that the computer had made some mistake, but she sent me back to Costuming to change into my Seas Costume for a 10:30 a.m. to 7:45 p.m. shift.

It was only when I got to the break room that I realized I had gotten the days of the week messed up: I had been operating under the belief that it was Saturday (again), when in reality it was Sunday. I didn't have the heart to see what kind of penalty I was given both for appearing a half hour late and in the wrong costume, but now I make sure that I cross the days off of my schedule, and quadruple check everything.

To recover from my lovely blunder, I made an emergency stop by the Basin store in Downtown Disney to get more of those excellent cocoa butter bath bombs that so relaxed me on my last program. They have worked their magic, and as I check my schedule for the umpteenth time, assuring myself that I really don't go in until 4:00 p.m. tomorrow, I can't help but feel a little less stressed about everything.

Kind of.

Chapter Twenty-Four

Amber Auditions for Her Close-up

"SO, WHAT IS GONNA happen is that I'm going to stand up here and stare at your face for about twenty seconds, and it's gonna be totally awkward. But we're going to play some awesome music to hopefully make it a tad less so."

When you say you work at Disney World, many people assume you're an entertainer. I have two friends who work in that role, and I've heard great stories about what it's like, so when I had some free time I decided to check it out. Lindsey had been talking about auditions since we arrived, and when she mentioned the upcoming auditions for princess-height women, I tagged along for fun. Disney doesn't exactly specify which character they're looking for, but since I was just going to experience auditions, it didn't matter.

Since I don't particularly look like any character, I knew going in that I would be sent home with the first cut. But I went anyway. I just wanted to have fun and do some serious people-watching.

Going was well worth it on both counts. It meant waking up ridiculously early and catching the bus, which I'm sure the Cast Members on their way to work thoroughly enjoyed. On the bus, I struck up a conversation with a girl wearing a *Les Miserables* shirt who spent the entire ride telling me her life's story, from her family's work with Disney to the fact that she auditioned for the little girl's role in *True Grit* to her current relationship status (confusing; they haven't said "I love you" yet, but there is always that anticipatory pause before hanging up on Skype).

Upon arrival, we waited in line, forming an even larger group of entertainment hopefuls. Stories were traded; for some this was their first audition, and for others it was as high as their third. Excited chatter filled the waiting area, as hopes hadn't yet been squashed into little tiny pieces.

The *Hercules* soundtrack greeted us as we moved into the room where we would be measured and registered. The group of girls I was with made it into the second group of fifty, and as we all sat on the floor and waited for the final person to sign our paperwork, the excited nerves that had previously caused so much chatter lulled the group into a bubble of silence.

When the evaluators stepped up to explain the audition process, our nervousness escalated to almost audible proportions. People were responding to the auditions in different manners: I, who honestly expected nothing, was gazing around with wide eyes (as wide as possible at that hour, anyway) taking everything in; my roommate was filled with butterflies and nervous energy; and others just wanted to talk with other people about how much they wanted this.

Sixty by sixty they let groups into a dance studio where, as promised, the evaluator awkwardly stared at rows of faces while popular dance music loudly played. Far from formal, the sense of disappointment afterward was still palpable. Leaving after just one name in our entire group had been called was much more awkward than waiting in a room full of 187 hopefuls.

The people I met — or even simply watched — in the few hours I was at auditions could supply a novel with a host of interesting characters. Even though I didn't interact with many beyond my small group, just observing them before and after the auditions was a unique experience that made me wish I could get a pass to attend all future try-outs. I feel as if I could sit, tucked away in a corner, writing up character descriptions the entire time.

You could tell the girls going to auditions, as they were the ones in yoga pants and sneakers. One of the girls, however, was so obviously aiming for Snow White that it was not even funny. You could feel her attitude from yards away; she had on the stage makeup, and a red flower pinned in her hair. It was so brashly apparent that it was off-putting. Waiting in line with a superior attitude, she seemed to think her spot in entertainment was assured. It gave the wicked part of me no small amount of satisfaction to see her walk out of our group with the rest of those rejected.

A disturbance rippled through the holding room as we were waiting for everyone to get signed in, and when I looked up to see what had caused so many whispers from the group, I saw one poor girl who had shown up wearing short shorts and a t-shirt that had been cut and tied above the waist. Some were scornful; others felt bad for the person who had come with no prior knowledge of how auditions went.

Others who received this strange mixture of scorn and sympathy were a girl who showed up with one of those dreadful orange tans and bleached blonde hair, hoping to befriend Cinderella, and a Hispanic girl with a thick accent (beautiful, but not French) who was convinced her destiny was to be paired with Belle.

And let's not forget the wonderful girl who regaled me with her life's story on the bus, and who continued with it into the audition room. On the bus ride back to the apartments, she nodded off frequently, jerking upright when the bus stopped or when her head made contact with her neighbor's shoulder. Others on the bus provided similar entertainment, but it would take far too long to write up descriptions of them all.

Auditioning is highly selective; I think about 11 of the 187 people who showed up made it past the first cut. But even if you're not serious about an audition, the experience alone is so entertaining that I recommend it. Getting your feet wet never hurts, and it's one more thing you can add to your list of Disney experiences that other people will never be able to say they've done.

Back in the work world, not much has happened.

I've played with numerous small children who manage to make even the most wretchedly boring days worth it, taken some great photos, and finally conquered the squeeze breeze cart without the slightest hint of faintness — twice!

I can add up how much three bottles of water will cost without the aid of a calculator, I lived up to my Donald Duck character from last year on Monday night dealing with one of my leaders, and I spent a week of sleep deprivation hanging out with my family after work every night.

The Florida storms are excellent; lightning is frequently on the horizon, and I really should start putting my raincoat in my bag instead of leaving it in my locker, which is a good distance away from my work location.

The recycling in our apartment has reached ridiculous levels, as all of us are too lazy to take it out. I spent my one-month mark here in Florida in bed all day having a Harry Potter movie marathon after waking up at ungodly hours to hear the Pottermore website announcement.

I'm trying to earn the vast sums of money I'm sure to spend on my upcoming trip to New York City by working as many spare hours as possible, no matter the assignment. I'm even on the lookout for a parade control shift at Magic Kingdom (call me crazy).

Fingers crossed for extra hours and no fainting spells!

Chapter Twenty-Five

Amber Handles a Drunk

AS EACH WEEK PASSES, I'm amazed when I look back at my schedule and try to recall everything that happened during the previous seven days. Events that feel as if they happened ages ago were merely two days past, and things that feel as if they were yesterday I wrote about last week.

This week has had some fun stories.

On Tuesday, I went to Magic Kingdom with my roommate, Lindsey. Flynn Rider's last day was Saturday, and we were determined to see him as many times as possible. Lindsey had already visited with Rapunzel and Flynn on numerous occasions, but I had yet to see either of them.

We planned to arrive as soon as the park opened, because the line to meet these two can get as long as the line for Soarin' (which is pretty long!). I woke up early, showered, made coffee and bagels, and even had time to fall asleep watching Wimbledon before Lindsey was awake and ready to go. We caught the bus to Magic Kingdom and found ourselves in place at 10:30 a.m. for the projected 12:30 p.m. arrival of Rapunzel and Flynn.

Lindsey had a tactic: we would swap back and forth. I would stay in line with my autograph book, and she would go visit some characters, then we would switch. She visited with Alice and got some ice cream, then I visited with the stepsisters (the photo of which mysteriously got deleted from my camera, which vexes me to no end), and then she went to visit a few other characters. By the time she came back, we were let in to meet Rapunzel and Flynn.

They have the most adorable setup for the meet. A large concrete table is in the center of the pavilion, in front of a raised platform, with coloring books and crayons available to keep kids busy while waiting for the fun couple. To get everyone excited, a Cast Member comes out and starts a dance with the kids around the table, and after the grand finale, Rapunzel and Flynn make their entrance.

They were the cutest couple! Standing alone, he would have his arm around her waist or kiss her hand. When screaming fan girls would come and take pictures just with Flynn, Rapunzel would oversee with crossed arms and a raised brow. They knew their story completely, too. When Lindsey asked why he was leaving, Flynn responded that he was recruited for an expansion of the Snuggly Duckling, and asked if he could bring us back anything from his journey (she requested a rose; I told him books).

With promises to meet them again soon, we left and resumed character hunting. We met with Tiana and Peter Pan, and chatted with random guests in the line with us. I suppose being an enthusiastic Cast Member shows even when not in costume. It didn't take too long before the parents figured out that we worked for the Mouse. In line for Tiana, two kids asked to have their pictures taken with us before the princess came out.

And that's what keeps me so darn happy with my job.

Thursday I had the day off, and decided to make my way back to Magic Kingdom to see Flynn again, this time accompanied by a girl from work. We arranged to meet in front of the Sword in the Stone at 1:00 p.m., but I had lost my debit card that morning, and then the monorail I took from the TTC made it only a few yards before crunching to a halt. It was 1:30 by the time I made it to the Stone, panting from a fast walk there from the park entrance.

Otherwise, it was an enjoyable day. We started out by meeting with Peter, who was absolutely fantastic. The girl I was with had not been on Peter Pan's Flight yet, so Peter gave us surprise FastPasses, which completely made her day; it was all she talked about!

We stowed them away and made for Rapunzel and Flynn's line. The line (which ends at the alcove where Belle used to come out and tell stories) was backed up to the smoking section near Sir Mickey's. It quickly dwindled when one of Florida's lovely rainstorms hit, causing a river that flowed over my ankles and chased off all but the most determined of fans (or the fans' fathers).

We spent the rest of the day happily meeting characters and riding rides. It ended with a lovely S'more from Frontierland, which we devoured as we watched the Electrical Parade.

Friday I picked up a shift at Mickey's Pantry in Downtown Disney. It was a short shift, but that turned out to be a good thing, as it's quite boring in that shop. I went early in the morning to Costuming to pick up my clothes for that night, and returned home to nap or eat (I don't remember which, but those are my best guesses) until it was time to leave.

When I arrived, it was to find friendly Cast Members who made me feel far from awkward. The store had changed a lot since I'd last been there, and I was drawn to the spices area of the store more than once. The hours were spent straightening placemats and coffee mugs, and asking the Spice & Tea Company man the best way to cook chicken.

Later, while stationed at the cart outside, a co-worker and I noticed managers hurrying over to the fountain next to Earl of Sandwich. Curious, we asked a passing coordinator, who told us that a child had gotten stuck in the fountain.

How this had been accomplished, I cannot imagine, but sure enough, a crowd had formed around the fountain, and we watched a red-bill cap bob up and down as the poor kid was being pulled around by his parents.

Eventually, they turned the fountain off, and sirens were heard as someone had called in paramedics to help solve the problem. I'm still not entirely sure how they managed to release the kid, but I figure that if his hand was wedged in the hole securely enough to keep it stuck there for twenty minutes, it must have been an impressive feat.

Saturday was a typical day at work. I was tired, as usual, having been up until 2:00 a.m. doing laundry so I would have pants to wear that day to Image. I got off at 7:30 p.m., which was way too exciting.

Cassandra (a co-worker) and I made our way to the Cast Member exit, we were stopped by a staggering gentleman. I felt torn between amusement at his condition and trepidation at stopping to answer his question. Clearly inebriated, he wanted help finding his way out, and he kept cursing: "I am so f'ing messed up, you have no idea how wasted I am."

He tossed his arms around our shoulders and leaned on us as we helped guide him toward the exit, and then into a cab. He told us about his dog, Amber, whom he hates, as she has psychological problems. I think he kept getting us confused, as he would be talking about how cool Amber was, and then rant about something to prove her mental disorder. We managed to find out that he was celebrating his daughter's twenty-first birthday, and had somehow gotten separated from the other thirteen people in his party. He had forgotten his phone at the house they were renting, and just wanted to get home.

Finally, after much staggering, cursing, and professions of love, Cassandra and I got him to a taxi. We had been shadowed the last bit by a security guard, who kept an eye on us as we made sure the man knew his address. We stopped by Guest Relations to let them know that the man was on his way home (in case his friends came looking for him).

Another security guard then asked why we were so far from our location. We told her that we had helped an intoxicated guest to the cabs. "Oh, yeah, I heard about that on our radio."

Cassandra looked at me. "How often do you hear that? We were on security's radio!"

Chapter Twenty-Six

Amber Deals with Disney Discontent

I HAVE NOT HAD time to take a breath.

The past two weeks have been some of the most hectic I've ever experienced. The previous week I was working as much as possible to earn extra money for my trip to New York, even picking up a shift in Downtown Disney. Extra shifts are a lot harder to come by in this program than they were in last year's program; they've now changed it so that, even when people are trying to give away their shifts, managers can restrict it to those Cast Members already within the area. Which is great, except that usually those people ask around first, and the Hub is more of a last resort. That means there is a plethora of shifts out there, just out of my reach.

I was also frantically trying to find someone to take my shift for last Sunday. I was leaving for New York City on Saturday, and while my managers took a more, "Oh, well, I knew you were looking forward to that trip" tone, I was incredulous at the thought of canceling my trip for one day of work. It's a side of Disney that I don't exactly see eye-to-eye with.

I found four people willing to take my shift at the Seas — if Seas is short people, on some days you can really feel it, as it's such a small staff anyway — but they were all denied because they were already working forty hours. While I understand not wanting anyone to work overtime, I was a little skeptical that they were willing to be short-staffed for most of the day rather than give someone willing to take my shift the hours.

Not much happened leading up to my trip; nothing of note, anyway. I worked as much as possible, fell asleep when I should have been writing, and then had to wake up at three in the morning to leave for the airport.

I spent a fabulous four days in New York City: seeing a show, sleeping in the street as my friend and I camped out for the Harry Potter premiere, eating hot dogs in Central Park. Words cannot describe how amazing it was. I would highly recommend that anyone in the College Program who isn't desperately saving their money take at least one trip while in Florida.

For me, it was a much needed respite, especially after the 4th of July. By the end of that day, I was no longer the happy, smiling Amber that I usually am at work; I was grumpy, I was tired of obdurate parents forcing their kids to "fly" around the bloody castle for a novelty photo when the child was crying, and I was not able to tolerate anything else.

The next day was just as bad; people were behaving in a less than intelligent manner, to phrase it as nicely as possible, and I was quite ready to go home and wait for school to start again. I returned to a sink full of dishes, which only improved my mood, of course.

But I came back from New York much restored, which was good, as I'd gotten home from the airport at about eleven that night, and had to be at work at ten the next morning. I was so sleep-deprived, I can't even put it into words, but I made it through.

The next day I was awake even earlier, at six o'clock, to meet with four girls whom I'd met at the Harry Potter premiere in New York. I managed to make it to Universal in one go, without my GPS (which is a huge accomplishment), and I spent the day in Islands of Adventure — mostly Wizarding World — hanging out with fellow Harry Potter fans. I went home with the intention of napping, as I knew I'd be up very late for the premiere of the movie, but found out that lines were already forming. I showered, donned my Harry Potter attire, and headed to the AMC Theatre in Downtown Disney, where my roommate showed up a few hours later with her father. We sobbed through the ending of our childhood, I drove home in a stupor, and then rose again early the next morning for work at eleven.

Sleep deprivation seems to be a running theme, and time seems to move slower. I found myself saying to my mother the other day that in some respects I would have preferred this to be a summer program; I'm not having nearly as much fun as I did on my last program, and staying home would have led to more benefits, as far as getting all of my general education requirements out of the way so I could focus on my major.

Chapter Twenty-Seven

Amber Rumbles with Her Roomies

"PLEASE DO NOT PASS your infant across the clam-mobiles. There is a seven-foot drop full of machinery between them. Please do not pass your infant across the clam-mobiles."

You hear a lot of unique conversation around the water coolers here at Disney World. Working at the Seas one day this week, I had run back to get a drink of water (yes, it was quite literally water-cooler talk) and two girls from Attractions were chatting about some … less than intelligent guests they had encountered that morning.

"Oh, you think we're kidding," one of the girls said to me as I snorted into my paper cup of water.

"No, no, I believe you." And it's true. Just when you think you've seen all there is out of people, when you think they can do absolutely nothing more to surprise you, they pull out some grand stunt like trying to pass their two-year-old from one clam shell to another, and you find yourself baffled all over again.

Like the hordes of people who never consult their Times Guide and so don't realize that the Imagination Pavilion closes at seven — and yes, it has done so for many years now. Or the ones who ask why all the clownfish have different sized fins, or why there are seagulls on the merchandise in the Nemo store. What is that concrete track thing that makes a loop around EPCOT; I don't remember it being there on our last trip. Yes, we spent the morning at Disney World before we came here, and we just got off Fast Track (I hate when people can't get the names right; a pet peeve of mine).

Luckily, though, not all of the guests are that thick, and many of them are devoted Disney fans. I was working on the EO cart recently when a family came up, the parents and three kids. The mom told them all:

"Now, I don't care what you all say, you are all getting a Captain EO shirt. Now, walk around this cart and pick you one out, 'cause you ain't leaving without one."

She had seen Captain EO when it first debuted in the 1980s, and was adamant that her children were going to love it as much as she did. We chatted a bit, as the EO cart receives very little business, and I love the chance to talk with anyone who stops by for a minute or two. We talked about how Captain EO receives minimal attention, and how awesome it was that she was buying all of her kids the light-up sequined glove along with their shirts, a few Captain EO posters, and some light-up sunglasses which I was so charmingly sporting.

When a fellow Cast Member came to send me back for a new assignment, I warned her that she was about to receive a large purchase from the most awesome family I'd met all day — or possibly all week — and the mother gave me a hug as I went inside.

That night, the girl who replaced me at the cart told me that all three children had demonstrated their impressive moon-walking skills after they'd donned their superstar gloves. I was envious that I'd missed that sight.

Recently, roommate drama has had a momentary flare-up. Lindsey (whom I share a room with) and I get along very well; the mirroring Harry Potter pictures that we taped on our walls and the Disney stuffed animals that we piled on our beds (although hers is much more crowded than mine!) aid that friendship. Others, however, haven't been so lucky.

Two of my other roommates work in Magic Kingdom; they often leave for work late, and don't return until the early hours of the next morning. They each share a room with someone from Entertainment; those people work fairly regular hours in the middle of the day, sometimes earlier, sometimes later, but never arriving home at four or five in the morning.

One night, the two girls in Entertainment decided it would be wiser to share a room. It made sense, after all; this way, the people with similar schedules would be rooming together, and wouldn't have to worry about waking up someone as they came in, or disturbing someone who'd just fallen asleep as they were leaving. They moved everything quickly and neatly; I hardly noticed that any change had been made until they told me.

I went to my room to watch a video on my computer. When it ended, I managed to catch the end of a row between two of the former room-mates. Apparently, it was a huge inconvenience on the part of one of the girls who hadn't moved that she had a new roommate (despite the fact that we all live in the same apartment). How she figured this, I'm not sure; she knew the person sleeping across from her already, she wouldn't have to worry about waking her up when she came in, nor being awoken just as she'd fallen asleep. None of her stuff had been touched during the move; in fact, the girl who switched out of that room left behind her TV, since her former roommate had become used to it.

"...You've never lived with other people before, you've never had a roommate, you don't know how this works. You didn't take into account how much of an inconvenience this would be on my part. You think this was an adult decision, but it wasn't; it was just stupid." — Insert slightly fumbled explanation — "No, I don't even want to talk about it right now. I can't talk to you about it. Maybe in a few days when I've cooled down, but don't even go there."

Perhaps it's because I don't particularly get along with the afore-mentioned roommate that I scoff at her condescending speech, but the aggravation caused by a simple switch of beds was blown out of proportion by someone considered mature enough to live on her own. Others may disagree; Lindsey thinks she is perfectly justified in her anger.

Whatever the justification, it only adds to the small voice that would rather enjoy it if my program were coming to a close and I was returning to school. Not that I would leave if I were given the chance; I have gotten to really like a lot of my co-workers, and I'm too stubborn (I think) to quit less than halfway through my second internship with Disney, but walking through Target's back to school display had me wishing I was ready to buy pencils and college-ruled notebooks in preparation for another grueling semester. Nerd that I am, I always wished summers were shorter, and around this time of year I am ready to return to school, no matter how eager I was at the end of the previous academic year to finish it.

The combination of a boring job that is way too easy, roommates that try my nerves and tolerance, humidity, and the allergies that have lately caused my ears to ache and my throat to swell — it's all creating stress, and the only thing that makes it tolerable is my annual pass to Wizarding World (where I can grab a butterbeer) and the knowledge that the money I'm earning at Disney will help to pay for my studies abroad.

I am trying, however, to remember that I still have a ways to go, and though that seems like a negative right now, it means there's time for things to improve. A new batch of people comes in next month when some of the current CPs begin to leave, their time here done.

Although I feel that I haven't slowed down in a few weeks, remarkably little has happened. I've worked, I've taken pictures, I've straightened far too many plush toys, and I've checked people out. I went to New York, where I finally met fellow dorks who know who Archie is and own magic wands.

Then I came back to work, mood buoyed by my travels, yet still more discontented with what I'm doing. I like new challenges, I like to keep learning. Maybe it's because I've done the program before that mars this experience; maybe I had a more challenging role last year (okay, that's a definite, not a maybe) and that's why I enjoyed it better.

The restlessness that set in about four or five months into my program last year has already kicked in, and I feel like I should be doing something more. Perhaps I'll make that my next project: finding how I can move about while I'm here.

Nothing truly exciting is on the horizon, either.

I'm starting research into the Worldwide Conservation Program for an article for *Celebrations* magazine, and am trying to focus on keeping my room clean for more than a day. I'm seeing *Harry Potter and the Deathly Hallows, Part Two* for a third time Tuesday before work with Lindsey and possibly a few others (though I have no idea who). And I suppose I shall continue to attempt to figure out what in the world I'm going to do when college is over, though I have a feeling any plans I make will be dashed before I even start my Masters program.

Oh, the life of the young, where roommate drama is the highlight of the week, and laundry sits in the basket for four days before it's folded and hung up.

I guess I'll just keep swimming. (Lame! But I've been at the Seas all day, and it just sticks with you, you know?)

Chapter Twenty-Eight

Amber Circles the Wagons

"EDMUND, BAD THINGS ARE going to happen if you send me out there. I didn't eat breakfast or dinner, I already feel ill, and my roommate woke me up at three in the morning to tell me a guy thought she was cute. It's not gonna be pretty."

It has been an eventful week, to say the least. I started it off by getting sick on Monday — yet again. I came in and felt a little woozy as I worked register 3 (which is on the rotation to go out to the EO Cart), but what can you do? I was hoping it would go away by the time my bump came and I had to go outside.

It didn't.

I was out there scarcely thirty minutes, and was frantically trying to figure out how to work the radio to page Edmund, the coordinator. At first I didn't get a response, and leant up against the counter for a bit, watching the lovely little stars float around. Luckily, the EO Cart doesn't get much business, so I didn't have to worry about a guest coming up to purchase something. By the time Edmund paged back, saying he'd been on the telephone, I was crouching behind the cart.

"What?" he croaked in his grouchy old man voice (he is frequently compared to Carl from *Up*, and I'd say it's an accurate description, for the most part).

"Um, yeah, I'm going to either pass out or throw up. Can you send someone out?" I could hear his annoyance in the silent radio. My friend from Attractions wandered over to see if I was alright.

"Yeah, yeah, just a little sick. I swear, Edmund is going to give me so much crap for this!" He stood there until Edmund came out with another Cast Member, pointed me to the bathroom, and told me to take five. I hurried to the bathroom and sat for a bit, but the feeling wasn't going away so I just gave up and went inside.

Where I was sent back to the cart.

My Attractions friend gave me an encouraging pat on the back as I made my way to the cart, and I was drinking water like no one's business while I waited for the rotation to kick in. I wasn't out there for more than ten minutes before I was sent inside to Theatre Sales (the person who stands beside the wall of photos with the clipboard).

Usually, when I go inside, I'm better after a bit, but this time I was still feeling ghastly. A few people commented, especially when I had to sit down for a few seconds when there were no guests around. Someone had brought a big bag of pretzels, and they sent me back to the closet to eat a handful. I consented, but not three minutes after eating them, the same person who had had to take over the EO cart while I nearly passed out was watching Theatre Sales as I walked hurriedly to the restroom to throw up.

I felt better afterwards.

Though I considered ER'ing (getting an early release), the stubborn side of me decided to stay for the rest of my shift. It was a good decision; nothing about going home would have made me feel any better than moving around and doing work. But I swear, before this program ends, I'm going to be the girl who always gets sick at work. It makes no sense; I don't get sick playing in the parks, and I've survived band camp without any incidents. Heat shouldn't be the problem. The only thing I can think of is that I'm just allergic to my job.

Work progressed normally, and then Thursday came around. Probably the best day I've spent here in Disney on my program thus far. I was telling a co-worker why I liked being busy, and how when I got bored on my program last year, I even went so far as to single-handedly construct a fort in the living room. Which got him all excited, of course.

And when minutes later I turned to talk to one of my other friends, Lauren, we started talking about food and carrot cake. Somehow, both of these conversations culminated in Fort Day, an all-day event that would take place at Lauren's apartment, where she, Chris, and I would bake, build a fort, and watch movies. Another girl, Grace, got in on the project, and we all assembled recipes and gathered blankets for the big day.

Around one-thirty in the afternoon I pulled into Vista, my car Dinosaur loaded with blankets, chips, and a bean dip that is absolutely wonderful, and my collection of movies (of which we watched none). Somehow I managed to get everything up to her third floor apartment in one trip, and while Lauren began baking cookies and preparing Oreo truffles, I tackled the fort. Lauren had already started it, but neither of us could figure out how to anchor the sheet to the window ledge. After much deliberation, I went out and checked the trunk of my car, returning with a quart of motor oil, another of power steering fluid, and a mostly used gallon of window spray. While not the sturdiest of anchors, they served their purpose as I sat inside the tent, linking all the blankets together with safety pins.

Eventually, Chris, Grace, and another girl from Future World North, Kristen, came in, following the sounds of the *Hercules* soundtrack we were blasting. It was a good thing I built the fort before they came, because clearly no work was going to be accomplished now that the whole group was there. Lauren kept having to chase Chris out of the kitchen as he tried to steal some chocolate, Grace was dancing everywhere, and Kristen and I were busy introducing ourselves, as I haven't been deployed to Future World North, yet.

The day was fantastic. We cooked (no carrot cake), ate junk food, and Grace made shrimp with rice and garlic sauce. We toyed with the idea of going to Beaches and Cream and attempting to eat our way through the huge, legendary Kitchen Sink dessert, but that idea was rapidly abandoned as we consumed even more junk food. The fort, which had been the central idea of the day, was quickly torn down after we all made it inside; it was large enough, definitely, but the couch that we were using as a backrest kept scooting backward as Chris leaned against it, and the motor oil anchor kept falling. And it was just way too hot for five bodies to be inside the little mini-oven the fort had become.

Movies were watched, balloons were bopped around the room and popped, and much fun was had in general. Around three in the morning, though, our energy was starting to peter out, and as Grace and I started to fall asleep where we were — she on the floor with a body pillow, and I on the couch in a nest of blankets — Lauren went into her room, gave each of us a stuffed animal, and we all situated ourselves. I was the only one who ended up not sleeping on the floor, choosing the arm chair to curl up in instead, and every blanket, sheet, and towel that had gone into the construction of the fort was used.

The next day, we awoke to Lauren making "muffins", which were really spice cake cupcakes. Kristen and I ran to Walgreens and got some orange juice, and we sat around on the floor goofing off, eating cupcakes — er, muffins — and dozing off.

Most people had work that afternoon; since Lauren and I were off, we decided to go to the World Showcase. After the group dispersed, Lauren and I spent the evening meandering about the Showcase, dropping into Restaurant Marrakesh for an early dinner and ending with pastries from Boulangerie Patisserie.

The week ended with another Harry Potter nerd-out session, during which I stayed in front of my computer from about ten o'clock until six the next morning, waiting for the Pottermore website to open. The group of us who'd met in New York all have a Facebook group, and we chatted nonstop until we had each received our validation e-mail.

As I type this, I should probably be up and getting ready for my wonderful six-hour shift, so I shall bring this entry to a close, get up, and have a bagel.

Chapter Twenty-Nine

Amber Exposes Disney Merch

ALTHOUGH I HAVE DETAILED the weekly personal events of my current stint in Disney's College Program, I just realized that I haven't yet explained what really happens at the workplace.

My role is merchandise in EPCOT's Future World West. This includes three primary locations (not counting nearby carts): Green Thumb Emporium, the Soarin' gift shop; Sea Base Alpha, the Nemo shop at the Seas; and Image, the gift shop for Journey into Imagination with Figment.

You've probably never heard of the Green Thumb Emporium, a one-register shop in the Land where the top seller is cotton candy that must constantly be changed as children squash it into a solid, unappealing mound. It's hard to accurately describe a shift at the Green Thumb. I have only worked there as a relief worker for whomever is taking a break. But I've heard that it's a tricky place. Most of the time, it will be boring to the point of insanity, more a post from which to people-watch than to bring in any real money, and then BAM! — you're swamped with guests.

Apparently, when the Brazilian tour groups were in last month, Green Thumb got very hectic. It's a tiny store the size of the Sea's storage room, and it was flooded with people who didn't speak English very well and who wanted to know the price of everything.

The thirty-minute stints that I've put in at the Green Thumb have gone by fairly quickly; you are mostly asked where the restrooms are (just around the corner), and for change to use in the coin press. Donations for Disney's Worldwide Conservation Fund are taken here as well, and while the daily target is only forty dollars, the Green Thumb receives so little business that it's hardly ever reached.

Sea Base Alpha (or Seas, for short) is my favorite place to work. Even though I'm usually freezing in there, it's the most laid-back of the three gift shops, and the one most likely to be busy. There's always a mountain of plush to be straightened, pucker powder to be cleaned, and jewelry to be sorted back into its original places. We keep a bubble gun in the closet to "Merchentain" with occasionally, and the music is much, much better than the rubbish they play at Image.

There are only three positions in this shop: two people on register, and one tasking (which means they are either stocking, entertaining the Guests, or straightening the shelves). I've rarely met an unhappy guest at the Seas; sometimes people are disappointed by our lack of Crush t-shirts or Marlin plush, but typically that is the extent of their irritation.

Each day the scuba leaders bring by a DVD for those who went diving that day to purchase. And at least one person comes in seeking the brochure about saving the sea turtles that Crush told them about next door. We have to explain again and again how to get to the Coral Reef restaurant ("out the doors, to the left, all the way around past the sea gulls and the ride entrance"), and the Worldwide Conservation Fund makes much more when you can implore guests to help save the sea turtles who've just been talking with them.

At Image, a shift can range from dreadfully dull, with absolutely no guests, to chaotically hectic as guests complain about pictures and threaten to fight over their spots in line. It has the most positions and the most people.

Registers 1, 2 and 4: These are the regular registers. You ring up guests as they bring you over-priced bouncy balls and their photo vouchers, do price checks on Legos, and then wander around the store and attempt to straighten things when it's slow. If the registers aren't busy and photo editing of guest pictures needs to be done, usually someone on register 1 or 2 will step back and help out.

Register 3: This is the most dreaded of the registers (though I know

Cast Members more afraid of register one, because they have to deal with showing guests their completed pictures). The person on this register is on rotation with the EO Cart and Theatre Sales, and very few people actually look forward to going outside to the EO cart. Registers 3 and 4 are also the hardest hit when it rains, as they're right next to the doors.

EO Cart: After you serve your stint at register 3, you get bumped to the EO Cart, located outside the Imagination Pavilion, and hope someone will stop and chat with you, because it rarely gets much attention. Occasionally, you'll run into a hardcore Captain EO fan, but usually people stop by to laugh at the sequined rockstar glove or inquire about the price of a squeeze breeze fan (they rarely buy one, though, at seventeen dollars). Most often you're asked for directions to Soarin' and the World Showcase, and that's about as exciting as it gets.

Theatre Sales: From the EO Cart, you're bumped to Theatre Sales, where you stand in front of the wall of photos and sign people up for their own photos. While it can be a fun role, interacting with guests as they walk by, you often end up serving as decoration: guests will look at the wall of photos, maybe nod at you politely, and then — despite the fact that they've watched someone else sign up with you, and completely ignoring the clipboard in hand — walk up to the people in the theatres and pester them with questions.

Theatre: There are two theatres, and neither of them really has any advantage over the other, besides one being more accessible for guests, which means they hover there, oblivious to the shorter line in the other theatre. It can easily be one of the most frustrating roles: trying to coax children to look in your direction and smile at the same time, dealing with demanding guests who want their photo to look just right ("no, no, up a bit. That's too far. I want it to be right there" — and typically poke the puzzle touch-screen and screw everything up), and unreliable software. But it can also be one of the most rewarding roles, as the high level of guest interaction ensures that you'll meet some interesting people.

Tasking: The duties for this role are greeting guests, creating a magical moment, or cleaning glass and straightening shelves. Cast Members usually take this to mean wander around; depending on the Cast Member, some actually do straighten and clean, but others wander over to their friends for prolonged chats.

Water Cart/Squeeze Breeze/Glow Cart: Our cart has been broken for a while, so we haven't had anyone go out to these positions, but from previous entries, I'm guessing you have a pretty good idea of what we do there.

Editing: By far the most popular position in Image, Cast Members on editing sit in the closed area behind registers 1 and 2 in really cool chairs and edit guests' photos. The detail Cast Members go into while editing varies: I'm a tad OCD, so I like everything to be edited as best as possible, though I'll speed up if we get behind. Depending on the size of the photo, editing can be a tricky process. (Fingers together is all I have to say. It is ridiculous, trying to get our editing tools in between guests' open fingers!)

I have also worked several stocking shifts. While at first the idea of being by myself for the day, opening boxes and hanging t-shirts, sounded mundane, I really do enjoy these shifts. On days you are scheduled for the heart of house (stocking shifts), you show up in your generic costume (the same blue and purple shirts and khaki pants we wore for training; you can wear them to perform any role in Future World) and clock in. From there, you are pretty much left to your own devices.

I've come in at seven in the morning to open and left at three-thirty in the afternoon, unpacking boxes that had been received by the six a.m. stocker. I have closed, coming in at two in the after-noon and wandering around our three locations to make sure they have everything they need throughout the evening. You take your breaks when you want them; sometimes you are required to go to the Land and give someone there a thirty minute break; sometimes you have to bring in the squeeze breeze cart and clean it for the next day's use.

Usually, though, the majority of the time is spent making lists — 3 medium purple Figment shirts, 2 x-small sweatshirts, 4 small uni-corn pops, etc. — and running back to the stock room to replenish whatever guests have bought.

My fear that I would be bored out of my mind was quickly allayed as I bustled back and forth. The shifts pass quickly, and it's quite refreshing to spend the day by yourself. If there are people working that I don't like (there aren't many of them, but goodness knows they exist), I can avoid them while stocking the store, then make my way to a location where people I do like are working. There's a level of independence to the role that suits me well.

And that's about all for my locations. All rather easy positions, all rather self-explanatory; but all capable of being underestimated.

Chapter Thirty

Amber Gets a Thank You Card

THIS TIME LAST YEAR, it was I who was packing my bags and saying my farewells. School was about to start, and I was being forced back into the real world without ceremony. This week, it was my turn to witness it from the opposite vantage point.

There isn't a huge difference between this bunch of CPs leaving and those leaving last year, other than that I was only here with these people for two months or so; last year, I was with people for five or six months before their time was up. I was definitely aware of the shortness of time, but that's not to say we didn't have some fun.

In my entire program last year, I didn't venture too far from Orlando. Actually, the only time I left Orlando was when I got lost one of those first few days driving back from Target. A little while ago, however, some friends and I made the spontaneous decision to take a trip to Cocoa Beach. I honestly can't even remember how we decided on going, but I do remember getting everything ready (sunscreen, camera, Powerade — check) and picking everyone up after my Adventures info-session early in the morning (more about that later).

We packed into my car. Grace, sitting in the passenger seat, DJ'ed, and we set out. The road trip was one of the best parts of my program. When we finally got to the beach and parked at Ron Jon's, it was already into the afternoon, but we found a relatively clear spot on the beach to leave our stuff. I put on some sunscreen, and we spent the next few hours immersed in the ocean, being knocked about by waves and swallowing way too much salt water.

Eventually, it was time to get out and find some place to eat. After a few minutes wasted trying to make a decision, we got in the car and drove, everyone calling out directions until Chris spotted the pier. We pulled in, heard the live band playing and smelled the seafood, and found a table. Starving after our day spent jumping over waves, we ordered massive amounts of food and tucked in.

It was dark when we left, laden with Styrofoam containers of crab cakes and fried shrimp. The drive home was just as fun as the ride out, except this time it was set against the background of an awesome display of lightning ahead of us for the majority of the drive.

My last few weeks were also punctuated by quite a few impromptu sleepovers, where conversations lasted long into the night and sleep overtook us before the urge to get up and make our way back to our own apartments. After one such night, we woke up around noon and decided to head to IHOP for breakfast. Our waitress was an amiable woman from Macon, and when she heard one of the girls in our group say that her goal was to pick an orange in Florida, she immediately gave us heavily-accented directions to the orange grove near her house.

We had planned on spending the afternoon moving things from one apartment to another, but when we reached the parking lot, I found myself turning onto I-4 rather than Little Lake Bryan. We drove along with no clear directions in mind, music playing and our random, sporadic conversation drifting over it. Somehow, we managed to find the place after driving around randomly — only to discover that it was closed until October 1. But we were having too much fun to turn around and return home, so we drove on for several miles, everyone in the car shouting out left or right when we came to a stop sign. Eventually, when we emerged from the arbitrary backroads and returned to civilization, I set the GPS for home.

That afternoon was spent casually doing whatever, as it was one of the last days for two in our group. After a quick stop at EPCOT to pick up stuff they had left for co-workers to sign, and some quick-service food in Mexico, we headed back to our apartments to regroup for our fireworks excursion that night. We drove to the Polynesian just minutes before Wishes began, and spent our last night as a group sitting on the beach, someone's phone playing the soundtrack perfectly in sync with the colorful flashes of light across the lake.

As far as work goes, there have been a few changes. I went to an info-session for the Adventures program; for the first time since 2008, Disney is hiring guides for this program. Since traveling is the one thing I am absolutely certain of in my future, I figured that Adventures would be a wonderful place to start; planning vacations for people and then leading them around places like Italy or England? What could be better?

After just two hours of sleep, I woke up, donned my business attire, stopped by Starbucks for some coffee, and made my way to the Contemporary. There I found out that, while it still sounds like an exceptional opportunity, the numbers aren't exactly encouraging. There are about forty-five Adventures guides for the entire program; when they last opened positions in 2008 (and they didn't even specify how many positions were available at that time), 12,000 people applied. As someone who doesn't speak another language and is not majoring in tourism or is a travel planner, the odds are slim. But since I'm fairly certain that I don't want to work for Disney again, it wasn't a huge upset.

At work, I was trained for hotel delivery and package pickup. It was a random training; apparently, one usually requests to be trained in that area, but I just had it scheduled for me, without any of my managers — or the managers in Future World North, where package pickup is located — aware of it. I turned up in the North and clocked in, and the manager, after figuring out that I really was supposed to be there, gave me vague instructions to wait for my trainer, whoever that would turn out to be.

After getting lost a bit (I hadn't been to the North since my training in May), I finally found someone who led me to the package pickup room, where I sat and waited. My trainer showed up a little late, completely unaware that she would be training someone — understandable, as she isn't a trainer. But she did very well, explaining things as I shadowed her around her normal day. It seems like a fairly easy job; it's primarily organization, which I love. Sorting and logging packages, going on runs and picking them up from the different areas in the park — nothing too difficult. Maneuvering the large delivery van is potentially problematic, as is the fact that I'm certain I'm going to get lost while navigating backstage, but I was assured that was totally normal, and all I would need to do is page someone at base and they'd talk me through whatever mess I got myself into.

The only downside to being trained for package pickup is that I'll be sent over there more often, limiting my time in the West. While I like the backstage roles — stocking is one of my favorite shifts, after all — I'll also be missing out on some of the guest interaction that reminds me why I like working for Disney in the first place.

Today, for example, I was taking pictures all day. A little girl of about three or four was getting her picture put into a puzzle with the princesses, but she wasn't having any of this smiling business. After quite a few pictures, hoping to catch one of the rare moments when she would be smiling in the direction of the camera, we finally, finally got a wonderful shot. Later, as I was waiting for the puzzlemaker to free up and was chatting with the next family in line, I felt someone tap at my leg. I looked down and the little girl was back with a card in her hand. Her family had made little laminated thank you cards for Cast Members who made their trip especially magical, and I was deemed special enough to receive one.

Chapter Thirty-One

Amber Counts the Days

I HAVE ROUGHLY SEVENTEEN weeks left on my program, as my mother reminds me every time I am on the phone with her.

While seventeen weeks sounds like a long time, the reality is that the weeks, as you experience them, are speeding by. Between work and going to the parks with friends and all other manner of activities, the time from one Thursday to the next (always Thursday, as that's when you get paid unless you're an international CP) is startlingly brief. They seem to rush by in a blur, so that I don't remember exactly what I did throughout the week, but am acutely aware that a large chunk of time has elapsed.

As I predicted, I am scheduled for package pickup from now until the seventeen weeks are up (I don't actually know this, but based upon my schedule since I've been trained for that role, it seems likely). Which is actually okay, because I'm quite enjoying my time there. I overcame my fear of driving the behemoth van, and now enjoy taking an hour to drive around backstage and pick up packages from the different locations. Two of the people I work with aren't such big fans of driving, which works out well for each of us, as they are always willing to take the Mouse Gear run (which involves pushing a big black bin around outside) while I or someone else drives for them. The rest of the time is spent logging in the packages and putting them in their places, which takes no time at all, really. Then we all just relax, lounging about in the two chairs, on the floor, or in one of the bins. It's a good thing that I like the people who work at package pickup; everyone seems to possess a laid-back air that makes doing nothing rather fun.

On Tuesday I worked my first ever shift at the Green Thumb, the gift shop outside Soarin'. It was raining when I arrived, which was wonderful, because that meant I had a steady line for well over two hours of people wanting to purchase ponchos and umbrellas, or candy to munch on while they hid from the precipitation outside. One of the largest complaints of people who work the Green Thumb is that it is so dull, especially as there's no one to chat with when the line disappears. I didn't run into this problem until well into the evening, as I was working the EMH (Extra Magic Hour) shift from 4:30 p.m. to 1:30 a.m. There's not a lot to straighten at the Green Thumb, which is what I usually waste my time doing, but I was never too mind-numbingly bored. It's not a shift that I'd want to do constantly, but once in a while wouldn't be a nuisance.

Thursday I hit Magic Kingdom again with Cassandra and one of her friends, Nancy. We went immediately for food when we arrived, and sadly chose the Tortuga Tavern in Adventureland. I vaguely remembered eating there once before, and my family vowing never to return, but I couldn't remember why that was, so I thought we may as well give it a go as Cassandra was craving Mexican food. As we sat at our table with the rain falling outside, staring at our half-eaten soggy burritos, Cassandra pointed out that the unappealing sodden mess in front of us had cost an hour and a half of wages. None of us were entirely thrilled with that insight.

We ventured to the Tiki Room next, as it is no longer under "new management". Afterward, we meandered around the park for a bit, until finally Cassandra and I left Nancy to hit up Ghirardelli in Downtown Disney for a shake. By the time we arrived it was late afternoon, the air had cooled, and the sun was setting. We sat at a table outside and people watched for probably an hour, commenting on the poor woman who walked by wearing a jean vest from the 1990s, and discussing work. When my milkshake infusion was only frothy chocolate at the bottom, and the cookie had disappeared from under Cassandra's cookie sundae, we wandered up to the West Side to visit the street performer (who was particularly attached to Cassandra, refusing to let go of her hand until she replaced it with a little girl's) before catching the bus back to the Commons for my first round of grocery bingo.

Paige, my roommate from last year, had often participated in grocery bingo, but as it was always at night, I was usually working and could never go with her. Which, I'm thinking, wasn't an entirely bad thing. The area in the Commons in front of the bingo room was packed when we arrived, and only got worse as time passed. Cassandra, who was able to peer around the corner into the room, reported that it was full of disco lights and Cast Members filming the crowd outside for Housing the Magic, the College Program television channel. Eventually, we were allowed in a few at a time; it was so packed that they had people waiting outside for an hour before seats became available.

We were given our bingo cards, found a seat, and waited as they filtered in the rest of the crowd. Then it began. It was a very loud, excitable game of bingo, and as I was already tired from our day at the park, I was less than enthused by the wave of people who would cheer as they matched the number called with one on their board. We played different versions of bingo (and here I was, thinking there was only the one), at which I was always a failure. That turned out to be a good thing, because as the night progressed and multiple people yelled *bingo!* at the same time, they had to perform in a dance-off in front of the room to determine who would get the most groceries. Some people really got into it, while others stood there abjectly, waving their arms about. There was such a demand to get in that as soon as you got a bingo you were asked to leave so one of the unfortunate people who had arrived later could come in and have a go.

Cassandra and I stayed for a little under two hours, and left before everyone else so we wouldn't get stuck inside the room as the masses of people all tried to vacate the building at once. The walk back to Chatham was particularly entertaining for her, as I was exhausted to the point of not shutting up. We managed to fit quite a bit of discussion into the short walk, which was to be continued the next day at work.

That next day at work started at 8:30 in the morning. I had a double shift on Friday; 8:30-2:30 at Image, then 3:00-9:30 at package pickup.

I had picked up the shift at Image, as it had been a while since I worked there and I was starting to miss the place. The day, as long as it was, passed rather quickly, though as soon as I clocked out for the night, I was pretty much dead to the world. I drove home on autopilot, not even quite sure how I made it back. Luckily, the next day didn't start until two, and it was, again, package pickup, meaning I wouldn't have to do anything strenuous.

And that's been my week! Nothing too terribly exciting is on the horizon, other than a trip to the barber shop below Magic Kingdom to restore my hair to its lovely red hue that has faded since I arrived. For now, I'll just enjoy my lovely days off and try not to think about how little time is left for me down here.

Chapter Thirty-Two

Amber Crashes in Japan

I'VE SAID SINCE THE beginning of this program that it felt different from my program last year.

Not only does that feeling still apply, it's intensified.

Whereas last year I wasn't ready to leave until I had about a month remaining, this time I have about 16 weeks left, and I am dying to depart Florida.

Some people I would miss. Some I would miss a lot. The majority would not keep me here for a single extra day.

I'm not sure what makes this program so different. Maybe it's the lack of family atmosphere that was so prevalent theme at the Electric Umbrella. Maybe it's that, rather than spend my nights after work on the couch chatting with roommates or playing *Lego Harry Potter* with Paige, I hide in my room because the noise level in our living room surpasses obnoxious more often than I can handle. Maybe it's the knowledge that if I were at home, I would be in school and getting the rest of my general education courses out of the way. Maybe it's that autumn is my favorite season, and while everyone back home is enjoying the drop in temperature and the impending coloration of the leaves, I'm still stuck in shorts and tank tops when I venture outside for more than a few moments.

Whatever the reasons (because I'm sure I've missed a few), I'm here until January, and as much as I want to go home, no purpose would be served in leaving.

September is a very slow month for Disney World. Park attendance has dropped dramatically, and that means less and less work for me to do. I can only thank the unknown scheduler who signed me up for package pickup, because while I cannot stand to be bored onstage in front of guests, I'm perfectly fine propping my feet up on a desk and reading the hours away in between driving to pick up packages. I've been given only one shift a week outside of package pickup; I make my way to the West to stock once a week. Food and Wine starts soon, though, so that should cause an increase of people in the parks.

Speaking of driving, the inevitable has happened. One of our vans, 64, was in the shop while they did something to its tire, and we had a loaner van with no rearview mirror to use in its absence. I took out the loaner for my usual run. Backstage at EPCOT has many alleys that we have to pull into and back out of, and so the lack of a rear-view mirror was inconvenient. It didn't really hinder me on the run, though, until I made it to Japan, my last stop. To get out of Japan, I usually back into an area between two freezers and turn around that way. I knew there were poles behind me that I couldn't see in my side mirrors, so I rolled down the window and stuck my head out. About that time, with a dull thud, I backed the van into a pole, knocking my head into the side of the window. I pulled forward and got out, walking to the rear of the van in a state of disbelief.

At first I didn't see anything, which made me elated, but then I saw a dent about five inches across in the metal of the bumper. I drove back to base with no small amount of trepidation. After unloading all of my packages, I made my way over to the manager's office to let them know. I was given a paper to fill out with details of the incident. The next day there was another round of paperwork to fill out because it was a loaner van. I had expected some kind of safety reprimand or something, but the manager in charge of package pickup told me that he preferred to fill out the paperwork and leave it at that. The manager that I had originally informed, though, had mentioned it in the closing report, so everyone who had anything to do with our area was aware of it now. If a higher-up came asking questions about discipline, then I would find myself in a little trouble, but otherwise I should be fine.

Automobiles just don't seem to agree with me lately. The other day, as I drove to work, my oil light came on. Dinosaur started to drive a little funny when I made it to the cast parking lot, and I called Dad as I made my way through Cast Services. I had a quart of oil in the trunk, and he informed me that should be enough to get me to Walmart to buy some more. There I put another two quarts in the car, but the oil light was on again before I'd even reached Chatham — not even a five minute drive. I told Dad I would call him the next morning after I checked the oil level. When I went out, though, it was to find the barest amount of oil on the dipstick, and a large pool of it underneath my car.

Needless to say, I will be taking the bus for the next few days.

Not much else of note has happened. I visited the barber shop in the Utilidor, which caused me no small amount of panic when I realized the woman who would be dying my hair was your stereotypical fake-tanned, fried black hair, gum-smacking hair stylist, who instead of using the formula my hairdresser at home sent me, brought out a color board and tried to convince me that the blonde would really come out red. Despite the trepidation that I felt beforehand, it didn't turn out horribly — although let's just say that's another reason I'm looking forward to going home.

Other than that, I've read some books, done a little shopping, and watched a lot of *Friends*. I've been scouring the Hub for extra shifts to supplement my 33-hour weeks, and have only managed to pick up one of them, so far.

Chapter Thirty-Three

Amber Joins the Bus People

ONE OF THE MAJOR perks of the College Program is convenience. Disney provides housing so you don't have to. They provide cable and water and electricity — internet, too, if you bring a router. And buses to take you to and from work, the post office, and the grocery store.

I had brought my car with me, so I used the buses as transport to and from work, but not for much else. With Dinosaur down, I've had to rely on Disney's American Coach buses to get me everywhere I needed to go.

They've changed the set up for the bus stop at EPCOT. One of the major complaints about this particular stop is that it's the site of incredible potential injury as everyone jostles and shoves to make it onto the bus — preferably ahead of enough people to actually snatch a seat. As I'm good at weaving in and out of people, this setup didn't really bother me; if you could judge where the bus was going to stop, and you could squeeze your way into the mass of people from all over the world, you were in. Now they've set up a queue, which works well. My only complaint is that if you want to sit and wait for the bus, you might lose out on a seat, and that when people in line decide to smoke — a big pet peeve of mine — you can't move anywhere to escape the fumes. But there's less stress involved, less shoving, and less invasion of personal space.

And of course, there's always the enjoyment of watching people dash for the bus as soon as it emerges from the revolving gates, regardless of whether there's a line or not.

I'd never had to take the bus to the store, but I'd imagined the inconvenience. I tend to buy a lot of food; not too much that I can't carry it up the stairs from my car all in one go, but a good amount. When I boarded the H bus last week to catch a ride to Publix to pick up some groceries, I had already decided to finally utilize my crock pot and make a meal that would last all week so I wouldn't have to return to the store for a while.

Let me tell you, for a wimpy kid like me, carrying a bag of potatoes, cartons of juice and milk, and all my other groceries was not easy. I managed to knock into quite a few people as I lugged my three bags through the narrow aisles of the bus. It was an interesting journey. But the ride to Publix wasn't long, and by the time I'd finished shopping, the next bus was almost there to pick us up. The Publix stop, unlike Walmart, where there are a few benches set up along the side of the building, isn't really organized as a stop; it lets you out near a sidewalk, and then you return to that sidewalk and wait for another bus to arrive.

Taking the bus early is a good idea; the last bus comes around seven for final pickups. Some times are more crowded than others; the bus I rode to Publix had a grand total of five people on it, whereas the bus I took back was nearly full.

I miss my car. I don't mind riding the bus to and from work, though I do like the convenience of saving an hour of my day to laze around rather than boarding the bus and waiting as it makes a few more stops on its way to EPCOT, especially when I have the misfortune to catch a driver's change or break. Then you spend about thirty minutes waiting at Vista Way while the driver disappears and someone else comes to check everything on the bus. It's a good time to catch up on podcasts.

Grocery shopping? Not so much fun without a car, but not unmanageable, as most people here do it. I've seen various ways to avoid carrying too much; some people take rolling suitcases that they load up, others bring massive backpacks (although that relies on your ability to pick it up in the first place).

But I like the feeling that if someone is going somewhere — Steak 'n Shake, Universal, the beach — then I can get there with them, no problem.

In two weeks, my parents will be down with a different car from home, and a trailer to take Dinosaur back to Tennessee to fix it for when I return for school. Maybe I'll continue to ride the bus to work, simply to save gas money, but I will be extremely glad to have my own wheels again.

Chapter Thirty-Four

Amber Feels
Sympathetic Vibrations

THIS WEEK WAS FULL of small adventures.

My adventures have to be limited this time of year. A $135 weekly paycheck tends to shrink your options, especially if you're trying to save money, however impossible the task appears. In an attempt to improve that situation, I picked up one of the scant offerings on the Hub, turning my Wednesday into a 14 hour day: stocking in the West from 7:00 a.m. — 3:30 p.m, and then a shift at the Seas from 4:00 p.m. — 10:00 p.m.

Stocking that early in the morning is always a struggle, simply because I am in no way a morning person, and the lack of a car means I have to wake up an hour earlier than I normally would to catch the bus. Somehow, though, I made it up, and there's something about walking around the apartment complexes, or EPCOT itself, in the early hours of the morning, when everyone else is still — enviably — in bed, that gives me just a little bit of energy.

I encountered a problem before I even started my shift.

Costumes. I had the pants for stocking, but not the shirt. Disney limits how many costumes you can check out in relation to your status; as a CP, I'm allowed to have three shirts and three pants out. With package pickup, the small shirts are extremely rare, so I hold onto any of those I can get, as I spend most of my time there. If necessary, I'll pick up a fourth shirt for whatever shift I happen to be working; as long as I turn it in within a day or two, it's fine. But

I had thought that I had the blue shirt required for the heart of house shift. I got to Cast Services, thinking that the hours for Costuming were from 6 a.m. to 6 p.m.; the sign outside the closed doors crushed that with a large number 7. I went back to my locker and scrambled my brain for a solution.

Could I walk to work in my tank top and work pants, desperately ask to clock in (you aren't allowed to clock in if you aren't in costume), and rush back to Costuming to get the appropriate shirt? Could I wear the costume I brought from the Seas? But no, that wouldn't work, because most of the seven o'clock stock shift is spent in Image. I was walking slowly down the halls of Cast Services, trying to figure it out, when I saw one of my fellow Cast Members from the West open the doors of Costuming and re-emerge a few moments later with a costume. Elated, or as elated as possible at six-thirty, I went to tug at the doors — which were locked. After a few moments of tugging futilely at the door and muttering under my breath, a passing Cast Member who had stopped to watch my efforts told me to knock.

A rather disgruntled Costuming Cast Member opened the door. I hurriedly explained my situation, and she allowed me to dash down the aisles and return to check out my shirt. Who said the Costuming Cast Members were always horrible?

I made it through the stock shift much easier than I did my shift last week.

There was no sleeping on my break, or dozing off when I sat down to pass a wave of nausea in the Land's stockroom. I ran around Image constantly doing something; I had the feeling that if I paused, exhaustion would catch up with me and I would be done for. I kept setting goals: in an hour and a half you can take your first break, in thirty minutes you get to do this, in an hour that. It went on like this until 3:20 p.m., when I carried my stuff over to the Seas so I could spend my last few minutes stocking there before taking a break between shifts.

I was hungry, so I bought a bag of gummy worms and sat in the hallway backstage and chatted on the phone with my mother before my second shift of the day. I have a feeling that the Seas is this location's version of Fountain View; I was really excited about shifts at first, but now the hours just absolutely drag by as the air conditioner assaults you with gusts of chilly air. Luckily, I was working with a Cast Member I get along with really well, so we spent the hours alternately straightening things and standing around bemoaning how slowly time was passing. It's become common practice to cover the times on the register with Mickey stickers, to rid you of the temptation to watch every minute of your shift peel away. It doesn't really help if you wear a watch, as I do.

The normal release time for the Seas is 10:30 p.m., but as the area was all-clear (meaning there were no more Guests in the building), we were able to clean up by 9:30 and get an ER (early-release) for 10. We walked to the money room, and then made our way back to Image with the manager, coordinator, and the lonely soul who had worked the Land alone that day.

I went home and slept.

Sometime during the week, Cassandra and I started talking about burgers. Not McDonald's burgers — none of that pre-frozen patty stuff. We were craving thick, real burgers with all the fixings and no kiddie toys.

On our next mutual day off, which just happened to be the day after I pulled that double shift, we went looking for one. I slept in a bit before we got started. Our goal had been to get a burger and head to Typhoon Lagoon, since Cast Members get in for free when it's not the busy season. By the time I was up and ready, though, burgers were the only things on our mind, and I met her at the bus stop to catch the F bus to Crossroads, where Fuddruckers awaited us.

Except that, as the Florida autumn rain began to fall, the bus passed Crossroads and went to the post office, instead.

I looked across at Cassandra, as I'd never taken the F bus before. She confirmed suspicions: that the bus was indeed leaving us here, and we'd have to make the trek to Crossroads on foot. After waiting while one of the ladies on the bus argued with the bus driver about not dropping us off directly in front of the building (one of the riders had several large cardboard boxes to send out, and the driver was doing him a favor), we stepped off the bus and stood under the overhang of the post office, hoping the rain would slacken a bit before we ventured out. After several minutes of cajoling the dark clouds, though, the rain persisted, so we gave up and started off. Cassandra had an umbrella, and offered to share its protection, but it wasn't going to cover both of us. I don't mind getting wet, and it was inevitable at that point, anyway.

Our burgers were well worth it.

After we'd finished them, we walked back to the post office and sat on the curb until we noticed the ants crawling up our legs. Suspicious of how long it was taking the bus to arrive, I called the clubhouse to ask about the bus schedule. We would have to wait another hour for the next bus, and it was switching its route to take it to Crossroads rather than the post office, as that had now closed. So we walked to Crossroads yet again, agreeing that any further plans for the afternoon had better be canceled. We decided that a movie and cookies sounded perfect on such a gloomy day, and perhaps a journey to Chik-fil-A, as it's buy one, get a second original chicken sandwich or nuggets free for Cast Member day.

Back in my apartment, I began making cookies while Cassandra went to her place to grab some movies.

I had told my roommates — only two were home — that I was having some friends over, and we were going to watch a movie. This prompted immediate results: they both stretched out on the couch and started discussing what TV shows they were going to watch tonight. I thought it a bit rich, especially as everyone's mattress is out on the floor of the living room from their sleepover that's been going on for about a week now. But I've gotten to the point where I don't really care to be in my apartment any more than I have to, so I texted Chris, who was at Animal Kingdom earlier for a Cast party that got canceled, and we all reconvened at his apartment to watch *The Librarian* and eat some cookies with our Chik-fil-A.

As a Cast Member, we get some pretty cool opportunities.

On Sunday, one such opportunity arose in the form of a guided tour of the Haunted Mansion. I signed up for two different dates, well aware that my will power in the early morning isn't exactly commendable. The tour required us to gather at the Magic Kingdom bus stop by six-thirty in the morning, which meant that I'd need to catch the five-nineteen bus to get there on time. I debated back and forth as to whether or not I was going to go, but eventually came to the realization that I would regret the missed opportunity. So, when five-nineteen rolled around, it was to find Cassandra, Chris, and myself on the A bus to Magic Kingdom, all of us half-asleep (or, in my case, I'm pretty sure fully asleep).

Only a small group showed up for the tour. Our manager brought some Munchkins from Dunkin' Donuts to provide us with some energy, and we made our way through the Utilidor to the Haunted Mansion, where we met our tour guide. She'd been working at the Haunted Mansion for thirteen years, and had built up a wealth of information. We got to walk the ride with the animations and everything going off, and it was really a very cool tour, despite the time. A lot of history is caught up in that ride, a lot of things that I wouldn't have thought of if they weren't pointed out to me. Little details that I had never caught in the numerous times I'd been in the mansion before were made obvious by her point of the flashlight, and the eternal confusion as to whether the stretching room is an elevator or not was solved when we got to lie down on the floor and watch the ceiling descend toward us. "Now you know what we do when we get bored around here," the tour guide told us with a chuckle.

After our tour, five of us headed to IHOP for breakfast before returning to our apartments for some sleep — except for the one unfortunate girl who had to head back out for work right after breakfast. I managed a three-hour nap before catching the bus to EPCOT for my package pickup shift.

The upcoming week holds promise. There's a double birthday celebration on Wednesday that I'm looking forward to, the Cast preview of the Food and Wine Festival on Friday, housing inspections, and of course, my parents' visit for one day to exchange cars and eat around the world.

Free food!

Chapter Thirty-Five

Amber Hooks Up with Her Parents

TODAY, I WALKED OUT of the door, and it was autumn.

And it was fantastic!!

On Saturday, my parents came down to switch cars; I would take my dad's BMW and he would take poor Dinosaur (whose missing seal on the oil tank has crippled him) home on a trailer. While the day before was quite warm, I walked out the door in long sleeves to sign my parents in to security and was actually comfortable. I have since retired my shorts, and refuse to wear them for the rest of the year.

My parents stopped by the Caribbean Beach Resort to check in and change from their 13-hour drive, and then they came to visit me. Mom and I headed to Magic Kingdom to pick up buttons and maps from the 40th anniversary while Dad switched out the cars.

It was a relief to be at the parks with someone who goes at the same pace and who likes the same things as I do. Mom and I walked around and enjoyed the autumn decorations that had been put up since the last time I'd been there. We headed for Colombia Harbour House to have a tuna sandwich, but the line was unbelievably long — out the door and around the corner. So we wandered around, both of us complaining about being hungry but too indecisive to choose anything. Finally, we stood in line at Casey's and found seating at the Tomorrowland Terrace.

Then we left; the park was a little too crowded for our tastes. We headed to EPCOT to meet Dad and make our way around the world.

The Food and Wine Festival is my family's favorite time of year to visit Disney World, and I have already made it my goal to try every single item (non-alcoholic, that is) around the world before I leave. As a trip without my younger siblings, we were able to try everything we wanted, several times over if we so chose. Desserts were a big thing for us—the pumpkin mousse and the lemon chiffon were some of my favorites. It was a little too warm to eat all that we wanted, so we reserved what we didn't eat for when my parents came down again in eleven more days.

Speaking of the Food and Wine Festival, the cast preview was Thursday. It wasn't exclusively for Cast Members; guests who were lucky enough to be in EPCOT that day after 2:00 p.m. could purchase food as well. It was chaotic; New Zealand wasn't taking cards, managers were in a tizzy, and all sorts of frantic activity was going on. But the merchandise was a lot better than it has been in the past few years, and the food is just as good. The short lines (especially compared to Saturday) were very nice, and my friend and I took full advantage of them as we wandered around buying lava cakes and escargot. Before long, however, she had to go to work, and I had to catch the guest bus over to the Caribbean Beach to show my ID card for the discount on my parents' room—no easy feat, as I couldn't remember where the check-in area was, and I got semi-lost walking around the resort.

Inspections were this week. I didn't clean that much for them, at least not the common areas, as I'm being obdurate and protesting the apartment's general state of filth. I came home fairly late after my adventure to the Caribbean Beach, put away the rest of my groceries, and straightened my room. When the inspections team showed up that afternoon, I had just gotten back in bed after making some strawberry oatmeal and popping in a DVD of Gilmore Girls. We managed to pass, even though our oven wasn't clean enough (and I've made it dirtier tonight with cheese from the casserole I made), and Lindsey and I were told to take down our things from the walls. After three notifications, they make you go to a housing meeting; this means that we can leave our things up for the next inspection, but will have to take them down for inspections after that. As I predict there will probably be only one more inspection, I'm not too worried.

That's all the excitement for the week.

Nothing terribly fun, nothing terribly out of the ordinary. I set off yet another round of smoke when I was defrosting some chicken in the microwave; someone thought it would be a good idea to shove all the plastic lunchboxes under the microwave, and the plastic was slowly melting. I get to go to Barnes & Noble sometime in the near future now that I've got a car again (thank goodness!), but I'll still take the bus to work.

Chapter Thirty-Six

Amber Dyes It Red

THE MOST EXCITING THING this week is that they have changed the laundry machines.

That's right. No longer are we using the little pay cards that were such a hassle — it took a five dollar bill just to get a card (which itself cost three dollars out of that five), and then you could only use cash to put more money on it. Now they have switched to card readers, so you can use your credit or debit card to wash your clothes. Which kind of sucks for those people who do as I've done in the past, and just load up the cards with money so you don't have to worry about it again for a while. Luckily, I kicked that habit, and my card only has four or five dollars left to use up.

All this excitement, and yet due to the rainy weather that instills instant lethargy in me, I have yet to make it down to the laundry room to witness said momentous event.

Honestly, the longer this program goes on, the harder it is to find things to write about. Should I go into detail about my roommates waging a passive-aggressive war against one of the other girls and refusing to take out the trash until she does so first? Or that somehow my measuring cup always gets put back in the pantry with oil residue in the bottom, making my rice stick inside the next time I use it? Or that no matter how many times I say I'm finally going to clean my room, it always ends up with more clothes strewn about the floor?

The thing is, a dull routine has set in that I just don't have the energy to break. Work, sleep, eat, clean a little here and there. Read. Then work again. And it's not even a lot of work — I'm not entirely sure where all of my time goes these days. Thirty-three hour weeks, and nothing all that productive to show for my time. It is kind of sad; I know that while right now all I want to do is go back to school and take some bloody English classes, at some point next year (probably during math) I will be wondering why I squandered my time here. Maybe I'll remember how completely unmotivated I feel at present, but I doubt I'll find that an acceptable excuse.

Even now I'm racking my brains to come up with some bit of interesting information, something those of you who don't work at Disney would find interesting. I doubt the revelation that we identify alcoholic packages with a little red dot on the green shipping forms fits the bill.

Two of my friends who did the program last year are making plans to come back. Danica, one of my roommates last year, applied to become a cultural representative, which means she'll be working in the Canada Pavilion (last year she was a life guard). The other is planning to take whatever he can get, though his preference is entertainment. Disney has its addictive qualities, both for guests and for Cast Members.

The moral of this entry, I suppose, is that time spent working for Disney isn't always exciting. There isn't something always happening. I'm sure others would tell you differently; I'm sure that right now there is a group of people out there always working, drinking, socializing, and doing god knows what else, and defeating the purpose of my so-called moral. But I just put on my work shoes, which still are disgustingly cold and soggy, and I'm rather distracted.

Auditions are coming up again, and Lindsey is persistent, if nothing else. She plans on spending yet another morning at Animal Kingdom, waiting with at least a hundred other hopefuls to fill just a few spots. This time it's character auditions, not face, but at this point, she has succumbed to the Disney addiction, like many others before her, and has found that her goal in life is to remain here.

There is something to be said about the addictiveness of working for Disney. I myself fell victim to it during my first program, which is largely the reason why I returned this year. Something about the combination of co-workers, your job, and working in the happiest place on Earth all culminate in one huge desire to stay here for the rest of your life.

It's really becoming noticeable now, as the wave of people who came in on the Fall Advantage programs have just over three months until they're sent home. Business attire is a common sight lately, as people are dashing off to interviews for professional internships and full-time positions. It can be a daunting task — one of the guys that I work with ended up sitting across a table from about eleven corporate Cast Members, elaborating on why they should hire him as a full-time Cast Member. Another friend has applied to as many professional internships as she is allowed.

It's as if Disney is its own black hole here in Orlando. People get sucked in by the pixie dust and euphoria, and it makes their previous lives seem mundane. I know it sounds more than slightly cynical, but it happens — to *many* people. Your life can be entirely on track, and then when you come down here and find yourself having so much fun in a work environment, you begin to doubt if you truly know what you want from life.

Some people stay and find ultimate contentment. One of the managers I work with has been with the company for fifteen years, and just now got moved to a corporate position. Clearly, he loves what he does. My sole condition to going on the program last year was that I return to school, because although I am a nerd and love school, the pull of Disney is not to be underestimated. Two people from my last program are still here with the company, and likely will remain with it for the rest of their lives. Most of my roommates want to extend their programs; Lindsey doesn't want to leave.

So fair warning. Some people come down here and it makes them reconsider everything. Some stay for a while, and decide that it's really not for them. That's why I'm glad I came down this second time; I've realized that this isn't for me. Others, however, have found their love of Disney refortified, and now find it impossible to leave again.

As far as my daily life goes, little has changed. I'm getting more days in the West now, which is a nice break from the monotony of package pickup, although I haven't decided whether I like being back. It seems as if hours will start picking up again — a good thing, since I'm not a fan of the hundred dollar paycheck.

My family returned at the end of last week, which was wonderful. I spent mornings in the parks with them, and then worked in the afternoons. Mom remarked upon the rather poor job the woman at Kingdom Kutters (the Cast Member salon in the Magic Kingdom Utilidor) did on my hair, and convinced me to stop by Target to pick up some hair coloring. On my next day off, I bought some stuff that said it was auburn — fairly close to the color of my dye back home.

With my mother's conviction that if my aunt can dye her hair herself, I can, I put on the cape and plastic gloves, mixed the color in the bathroom, and felt like a complete fool squeezing red goop into my hair. I was a little wary of just how red the dye looked, but at that point, there was nothing I could do about it.

About fifteen minutes later, when I emerged from the shower where I'd rinsed everything out, I refused to look in the mirror until I'd blow dried my hair.

I looked like freaking Ariel from *The Little Mermaid*. Bright, anime red hair. It was brilliant. And not at all in the Disney Look. When I called my mother to tell her exactly how her advice had turned out, she didn't take it as seriously; she even told me that one of my friend's reactions (*Fix it. Fix it now.*) was a little extreme. And then she received the picture. "If I were there, I'd bring you about a pound of chocolate and some bleach."

The next morning I woke up early to venture to a salon I'd noticed behind my Barnes & Noble out on Sand Lake Road. I got there at ten — I didn't have work until three, so it should be plenty of time — and walked in, hoping they'd be able to fix the damage I'd done. Thankfully, when I pulled down my hair and showed them just how bright it truly was — think Coca Cola red, Pikachu's cheeks red — and they learned that I worked for Disney, they found time.

Four and a half hours and lots of money later, I less resemble an animated character, and could go to work without fear of being sent home.

Chapter Thirty-Seven

Amber Defects to Universal

IT'S BEEN A FAIRLY busy couple of weeks.

Whereas of late, the days have been creeping by, now they have sped up — whether that is due to my awareness that I now have less than two months left, or I've found more to do, I'm not sure. Whatever the reason, I still can't decide whether I'm glad of it or not. Part of me is absolutely thrilled that it's almost time to return to school and start working toward something again, and part of me is still sure that there are things I'm going to leave undone.

A few months ago, I bought an annual pass to Universal Studios. Not that I actually like Universal Studios — I can't stand SpongeBob or *The Simpsons*, I'm not really into comic book characters, and I possess an unnatural loathing for Dr. Seuss — but I felt, as a Harry Potter nerd, it was necessary. I haven't really had a chance to go there much, but last Monday, one of my roommates, Christina, happened to get a free ticket to Universal, and wanted to use it at Wizarding World. Who am I to refuse the company of someone who will spend all day wandering the replica-streets of Hogsmeade?

We woke up early so we'd get there just after opening, and following the back-road directions I've got written down in some compartment in the car, we drove to Universal.

It was a beautiful day; clear blue skies, not too hot, but still warm enough that the shade wasn't uncomfortably chilly. We made a bee-line for the Forbidden Journey, and while we had to wait a good thirty minutes in the greenhouse because the ride had broken down (it tends to do that a lot), we knew that as soon as we left the line, it would start up again, this time with a wait of an hour.

After that, we meandered through the crowded stores (really? did they not think that lots of people would want to buy ridiculously expensive Harry Potter merchandise?), watched the performances, and sipped butterbeer. We ate at the Three Broomsticks, watched the Ollivander's ceremony for the first time (a tad too corny for my taste; the dialogue was taken straight from the movie), and I restrained myself while Christina shopped away. We met up with some other Cast Members to ride a few rides, but they left to explore the rest of Universal, while Christina and I carried on with the magic.

By six that evening, we had done everything, been in the stores multiple times, and our energy was flagging. After Christina spotted two of the cast from *Vampire Diaries* and followed them to ask for a photo, she was ready to finish buying all her stuff and leave.

As if that weren't enough excitement for one week, on Thursday Chris and I decided to visit Cocoa Beach again. After the last trip there with Lauren and Grace, I realized how much I missed it. A chance day off together, with good weather, was a perfect excuse for a mini road trip. I woke up early that morning to drive to Universal — yet again — to pick up a ball cap from Margaritaville; I had forgotten my debit card when I went with Christina, and apparently I'm not allowed to let sun touch this red hair of mine. If I was going to spend the money on a ball cap, I wanted a Parrothead one. While I was on my way to the shop, I decided that, you know, the single rider's line for Forbidden Journey really is quite short, and Chris probably wouldn't wake up until the afternoon. So I made my way straight to Hogsmeade, yet again, and jumped in line. Once I'd had my fix of magic for the day, I stopped and bought a pumpkin juice and some exploding bon-bons, and picked up my hat on the way to my car.

By then, Chris had woken up, so I went home and we prepared to take off. Lauren had sent him a gift card to Dunkin' Donuts for his birthday, so our trip began with a stop at the Dunkin' near Vista Way to pick up a dozen donuts and some coffee. The road trip did nothing but make me miss Dinosaur — this new car has no cassette player, so my iPod adapter didn't work, it didn't have the convenient change drawer next to the steering wheel that I use for change at toll booths … it just wasn't my car. But once we reached the beach, it didn't matter. I camped out on the sand, because it was far too chilly for me to get in the ocean, but I did clock some good reading time. Chris alternated between chasing the waves and building mediocre sand castles. At some point I dozed off, and woke up quite contentedly to a near-empty beach and the stars emerging in the sky.

Work has been fairly consistent. I made a voyage back to West for three days, and it was wonderful to actually work with people that I'd only been able to say hello to previously. Now, of course, I have no time over there in the foreseeable future, but I am on the lookout for shifts.

I got reprimanded at work for reading at package pickup. This I have a problem with, only because we are done with all the work by nine o'clock, and have to sit in the empty room for an hour and a half with nothing to do other than stare at the tiles on the floor. Which is perfectly fine, apparently; no one ever gets yelled at for doing nothing when everything's finished for the night. But pull out a book to read during that time, and it's interfering with work.

I try not to sound bitter when stating my side of the argument, but it hardly ever works. My point is, that if it's perfectly fine to text or stare at each other when there's nothing to do, why is reading worse? I'm sorry that a book isn't as convenient to shove into my pocket not-so-covertly when you walk in the door, but is my reading distracting me from doing my work? No, because there's nothing more to be done than wait for someone to ring the godforsaken bell, and then it's easy enough to put the book down and go answer it. Granted, the manager had just come from confronting another Cast Member who was actually hidden away in a completely different room doing her schoolwork, and most probably had an attitude when he confronted her. But I resisted the urge to be a smart ass and held my tongue, and have made peace with the likelihood that I will get written up for reading before I leave.

I had a few things to look forward to soon. At the end of the week, three of the girls that I met in New York City were coming down for Universal's Harry Potter event. Unfortunately, I did not make enough money to buy the overpriced tickets (another thing, I was making twice, or three times, as much money last year; tip: don't choose merchandise if you wanna make money). Still, the prospect of seeing them again is absolutely wonderful.

And on November 16, I'm attending a wonderfully nerdy concert at the House of Blues. I'm a big fan of a group called Team StarKid; I'm not sure that any of you will have heard of them, but they are basically a group of university graduates, all theatre kids, who have made a variety of splendidly geeky musicals. They got popular with *A Very Potter Musical*, and one of their co-founders, Darren Criss, has reached mainstream popularity. I, however, am a fan simply of their musical talent, their humor, and the fact that they're just a group of nerds having the time of their lives. Their opening act is Charlene Kaye, who is a magnificent artist as well. Yes, I am attending said concert solo, but as my mother says, it's best to view it as "you have the confidence to do these things by yourself, which most people wouldn't. It's not that you're being a loser [my term for my habit of doing things by myself], but you don't need other people to have fun."

Honestly, I'm just hoping I get a picture with them.

Chapter Thirty-Eight

Amber Fails Inspections

IT HAS FINALLY HAPPENED. The inevitable has come to pass. We have failed inspections.

After my cleaning boycott, when I decided I was going to quit cleaning up things that weren't mine, I knew this day would come. Inspections were coming up; I knew they were. But I wasn't going to touch anything but my half of the bedroom and our bathroom. I had already scrubbed everything in the bathroom, and then the night before inspections I cleaned and uncluttered my half of the room before falling asleep.

I woke up the next morning to the sound of a whistle in the living room. The maintenance people had come early in the morning to install new faucets and showerheads — more eco-friendly faucets. I fell back asleep rather quickly, only to be woken up what felt like a few minutes later to people knocking on the bedroom door, and the clicking of a camera taking pictures of the illegal posters my roommate and I have on our walls. I feigned sleep, as I honestly did not feel like dealing with these people who were storming in and out of everyone's rooms, taking pictures and speaking in code, like we weren't allowed to know just how poor a state our apartment really was in until the last moment.

After I'd dozed off for a bit, I heard them explaining something to Jordan, who sounded rather terse in her replies. Lindsey and I looked at each other warily because we knew something was amiss. After about ten minutes of preparing ourselves, we walked out to see that we had failed inspections. And not just half-heartedly. No, we really failed. Everyone's bathroom failed but ours, the kitchen failed, the floors failed, the bedrooms all failed. The patio passed, and that was about it. Jordan stormed around on the phone, ranting about how ridiculous it was — ridiculous that we each had to pay a cleaning crew $25 (withheld from our next paychecks) to come and clean the apartment, ridiculous that we had failed, ridiculous that they had taken pictures of everything — while the rest of us just didn't care. And I have to admit, I wasn't too entirely fussed about failing, either; though I was upset at the $25 cleaning fee, which is now, like, a quarter of my paycheck.

Part of failing the inspection is that you have to undergo a second inspection a week later. Ours is approaching, and the apartment is back in the state it was in prior to the first inspection. The floors are a mess, there are more fast-food wrappers on the living room table, and I can't be bothered to wash my dishes because that means finding a place to put all the dirty dishes that are piled in both sinks. If we fail this one, we have to have a meeting, though I hope it won't come to that. I'll clean my own room again, maybe sign out a vacuum from the front desk, and make sure the kitchen floor is swept. We'll see how it goes.

I picked up a shift at the Emporium last Friday. The Emporium on Main Street in Magic Kingdom was my requested work location when I interviewed for the College Program. A few days before the shift, which was from 7:30 a.m. — 4:00 p.m., I went to scope out the place. I made my way through the Utilidor, came up on the wrong side of Main Street, and asked two older women where I would have to clock in. They told me to look for staircase 19, and I ventured back into the tunnels. It wasn't as complicated as I had thought. I went to the costuming building to pick up my lovely floor-length, brown-and-blue plaid skirt; puffy-sleeved cream shirt with lace collar; and a rather stifling tie that wouldn't adjust. It didn't actually look half-bad, though something on the inside of the collar chafed against my neck throughout my shift.

The night before, my roommates — namely, Christina, as per usual — decided that it was another night to scream for hours. And hours. As I was lying in bed, trying to sleep, I listened as four of my roommates, as well as three other people I only vaguely knew, conversed loudly in the living room. I was so thoroughly angered by their lack of common decency, I thought I was going to reach my breaking point, but didn't. I know I'll have to say something next time; there are only so many nights that I can stand to be kept awake for hours on end when I have to work the next day.

By the time my alarm went off, Lindsey was just walking in from the living room. As I sat up groggily, she crawled into bed.

It was an unexpectedly cool day, and I was wishing I had put on leggings under my skirt as I waited at the bus stop. The A bus arrived, and I listened to my iPod, more alert than I had expected. At the Emporium, I found the lockers and the CDS without problem, and settled in the break room to wait out the extra thirty minutes that I had given myself in case I encountered any problems. When it came time to clock in, I found a coordinator in the office who explained everything about the Emporium. The morning was fairly slow, but I was rather enjoying the atmosphere of Magic Kingdom. Christmas music was playing (not that I'm a huge fan of Christmas music, but it went well with the decorations), and everyone was cheerful and quite willing to answer any questions that I had. When I came back from my first break, I ran into Taylor, a coordinator from my area in EPCOT. That was quite unexpected, but apparently he picks up shifts at the Emporium whenever he can.

The shift went by at a steady pace, and I really enjoyed all of it. I chatted with a leader who gave me a GSF (Guest Service Fanatic) card at the end of my shift, acknowledging my willingness to learn and my eagerness to be in a new environment. I definitely want to work there again.

There was a bit of excitement after my shift at the Emporium; some of the girls I had met at my camp-out for the Harry Potter premiere in New York City were in town for the convention at Wizarding World. We were supposed to meet up at City Walk to watch *The Chamber of Secrets* at a theatre, but at the end of my shift they texted me that some stars from the film were meeting at a local Walmart to sign autographs. I immediately regretted my decision to not drive to work, and was anxious the entire bus ride home. I quickly changed and sped to the Walmart. After two hours in line, we were screamed at by a manager that there was absolutely NO WAY we were going to make it in the line to get autographs, so I and the people near me snuck around, took a few pictures, and threw in the towel. I'll try again next year at the convention in Chicago.

Work has seen a bit of excitement as well. I was working a shift at Gift Stop, probably the slowest store in EPCOT. It's the one at the very beginning of the park, outside the gates, where you pick up your packages. The night had been crawling by, when all of a sudden some little kid starts bawling. He had tripped over something and bashed his head on a ledge. Already the bump had swollen to the size of a ping pong ball. I wasn't quite sure what to do, but one of the guys in package pickup had me call 911 and wait with the boy. He was six years old and rather annoying, for all that he had just hit his head. The mother had a panic attack while the paramedics were there, the kid refused to keep the ice on his head, and the paramedics were getting fed up with both of them.

Later, during my shift at the Seas, a guest ran into the store and told us that a kid was bleeding in the shark room (which features a playset with the giant Bruce). One of the girls I was working with had absolutely no idea what to do, and the other was already faint at the sound of blood. She held the phone in her hand without knowing who to call.

Thankfully, after the stint at Gift Stop, I knew what to do. My experience with emergencies at the animal clinic kicked in, and I had her call 911 while I went to get information from the guests. I got the kid's name, age, what had happened, and whether or not he had lost consciousness at any point. I found the mother on the floor with the boy in her lap. He was three years old, and the baby wipe that the mother was holding to his head was already quite bloody. I went back to the register with her information to call a manager, and when he arrived, with the paramedics right behind, I stayed in the shop while the crowd of Cast Members gathered around the family. After all the drama was over, the manager for our area came over to give me a GSF for a calm and effective response in an emergency, which honestly made me feel quite good.

Both of the boys were okay, by the way.

Chapter Thirty-Nine

Amber Enjoys a Turkey Leg

THE HOUSE OF BLUES. It's a popular place for CPs. I never quite understood the appeal of it, but then again, I'm not the partying type.

But on November 16 I was sitting on the sidewalk outside the House of Blues, and I found myself reminded of my New York adventure. Only this time, I was solo, it was less than a couple of hours spent waiting on the ground, and these were StarKid fans. The time for the concert had finally rolled around, and I had showed up at Downtown Disney super early to get as good a spot as possible.

While in line, I met two local girls, Lynell and Courtney, and spoke with them quite a bit. Before we went in, we exchanged email addresses and Facebook information, promising to upload any and all pictures we got that night. Lynell frequented concerts at the House of Blues, it turned out, so I looked to her for the best way to hit the merchandise table and get a good place to stand for the concert.

Which was fabulous. Absolutely fabulous. Afterward, Lynell and I headed outside to wait for StarKid and Charlene Kaye to come and take pictures with everyone. Lynell didn't have a camera with her, so I offered to share mine, and just tag her in all the photos afterward. We made the rounds, and when the bus driver honked the horn to herd everyone onboard, Lynell and I parted ways. As I was still annoyed by the whole roommate situation, I bypassed my apartment to head over to Chris' instead, determined not to let anything ruin the happy buzz I was still experiencing from the concert.

The Food and Wine Festival was ending soon. I had not met my goal of eating everything in the little menu passports you could pick up at the stands, but I had tried most of it. I had gotten into the habit of going to EPCOT early, before a shift started, and stopping by at least one or two stalls before changing into my costume for work.

On one of the last days, Chris, YanYing, and I went to enjoy the Food and Wine Festival. Chris had signed up to work the Festival, but ended up withdrawing from the position and going back to work in the West; he enjoyed being a trainer more than he did selling beer to guests — not to mention that managers were all over the place during the first few days of the Festival, whereas they were rarely seen in the West.

His roommate, Manual, had stuck it out, though, and we stopped by one of the merchandise locations to say hi. Manual normally worked in Animal Kingdom on Discovery Island, but had volunteered to work the Festival — something any College Program participant could have signed up for. In fact, many times I found myself wondering why I didn't sign up to work it myself.

YanYing, Chris, and I wandered around, stopping whenever something sounded good like the salmon in Canada or the lamb from Morocco. When we stopped and sat on the curb in the United Kingdom so YanYing could eat her fisherman's pie, I mentioned that I had the phone number for the phone booths just across the sidewalk. Chris passed the time waiting for someone to approach a booth, then dialing the number and watching their reactions when they realized they were talking to a real person.

November began, and Chris and I decided it was time for one more beach trip. This time, we went to Clearwater instead of Cocoa Beach — partly because we hadn't been to that beach before, and partly because there were no toll booths on the way there. We both took pictures of the temperature readout on the dashboard; 92 degrees in November was a rare event for both of us.

Sadly, the warm weather was only present on the ride there, and after about two hours of watching Chris dart into the freezing water, I was wishing I had brought a jacket. The sunset, though, was spectacular; I've got shots down the beach of many other beachcombers standing at the edge of the water, cameras directed toward the orange sun sinking behind the line of the ocean. We did stay to watch the stars come out, but quickly retreated to the car, and the heater.

My family came down once again for Thanksgiving; I think they enjoyed that I was living in Florida more than I was, because it gave them a wonderful excuse to visit as often as possible. I spent most of the week they were here exploring the parks with them before and after my shifts. I never asked for any days off; they knew I was going to be at work, and they knew that I would be coming home soon, anyway.

Thanksgiving that year was definitely one of the more unique affairs we've ever had. I had the day off, and we spent the morning at EPCOT. Our Thanksgiving lunch consisted of fish and chips, with seagulls lurking around our benches waiting for someone to drop something. We had a sibling competition on the Kim Possible excursion: Jeremy and I raced Matthew and Hayley to see who could finish two missions first. We'd done this before, and Matthew and I had won (though, admittedly, maybe it wasn't a fair win). We picked up our Kimunicators in Italy, and then sprinted off in the direction of our first mission. I do not run very often, but this was an unfair competition: the two athletic siblings against the most unathletic and the youngest. So I did my best to sprint behind Jeremy, although by the time we made it through our first mission in Germany and were on our way to Mexico, I had to wave him on as I stopped to catch my breath.

About ten minutes later, Jeremy and I looked up from where we were lying on the ground between the East and West Towers to see Matthew and Hayley walking quickly to our agreed-upon meeting place. They accused us of cheating, and we had to repeat what our clues had been on both missions to satisfy their suspicious natures.

At some point we went back to the hotel to rest before dinner at Boma. Jeremy said he was starting to feel sick, so when we all packed into my mother's car to head to the restaurant, he was forced to sit next to the window, just in case. That turned out to be a good decision, as not even five minutes out of the hotel parking lot, we were turning around to take Jeremy back to the hotel, Dad staying behind to watch him while the rest of us went to Hollywood Studios for dinner instead. We still had turkey on Thanksgiving, it turned out, but in the form of turkey legs. The Osborne Lights were on display by now, so after our dinner at Sunset Ranch, we made our way over to the Streets of America, wrapping up the night with dancing in the streets and hot chocolate.

The rest of my parents' visit was spent touring the parks and resorts, and hunting out the different Christmas decorations. When they left, it was with the promise to return in a few weeks for Christmas.

Work was picking up a little, finally. Package pickup had been extremely slow, especially in the time between the end of the Food and Wine Festival and Thanksgiving. School's in session, which means fewer guests buying things they want sent to the front of the park or delivered to their resorts. Runs took only as much time as was needed to drive to each location and pick up the one or two packages typically found there. But with the approach of the holidays, the flow of packages was growing. I was grateful for that, because it meant less chance for me to get caught reading at work during downtimes.

Chapter Forty

Amber Seeks Holiday Cheer

"THERE ARE SO MANY people, Amber! So many!"

I would assume it's fairly common knowledge that Disney films their Christmas events ahead of time, way before airing them on Christmas morning. As Cast Members, we were able to find out what was happening each day, and do our best to catch a few of the events. Some, like the parades, were much more difficult to get into. Despite that, Cassandra and I made our way one chilly morning to Magic Kingdom, standing with masses of other people in front of the Castle stage.

We were there for the filming of the musical events. Neither of us was quite sure who we would be seeing, or if we would even know who they were. Both of us, however, were praying fervently that the rumors of a Justin Bieber appearance were false.

Standing in the crush of people, we received instructions from an enthusiastic man with a microphone telling us how and when to scream and clap and sing along. Scotty McCreery, a country artist I had never heard of, came onstage first, and I was pleasantly surprised by how much I enjoyed watching him. We saw him perform the same song a couple of times, the crowd screaming whenever they saw a camera pointed in their general direction. There was drama in between acts during the question session, when someone in the crowd pointed out that a star on one of the trees was crooked. Two men promptly came onstage with a ladder and righted the star, which soon slumped over again.

Cee Lo came out next, and unfortunately, I was starting to feel faint. Totally shocking, right? We watched Cee Lo go through his song once or twice, but he was less able to hold our attention than Scotty had been. Cee Lo had taken thirty minutes just to get on stage, and Cassandra and I had the feeling that his song would take more run-throughs than the previous performance. So we headed back to her car and drove to the area around Vista Way, where we had salads for lunch, and then made our next stop of the day: mini golf.

During the holidays, Cast Members receive little pamphlets of discounts and coupons. These include a greater discount on resorts, certain restaurants, merchandise … the Christmas holiday is a good time to work at Disney. Our booklet also included free rounds of mini golf. So after lunch, Cassandra and I made our way to the Winter Summerland mini golf course near Blizzard Beach, the Christmas theme fitting well with our day. The course was pretty much deserted, and we made our way around the holes slowly, taking an excessive amount of photos and trying our best to get our balls into the holes in a respectable time frame.

After Winter Summerland, we decided we had had so much fun that we drove to the Fantasia mini golf course. It, too, was fairly empty, and we had an absolute blast as we incompetently did our best to keep our balls on the course. At one point, poor Cassandra's ball ricocheted off one of the fixtures and into the stagnant water, and she laughingly complained as I got photo documentation of her fishing her ball out of the water. At the end of the course, we asked a man to take our picture in front of the Sorcerer Mickey statue that served as the last hole. He assured us that we had picked the most qualified man for the job, that he took excellent pictures — looking at the photo after he had handed the camera back and walked away, we both agreed that he was a complete liar.

We ended the night by picking Chris up from EPCOT after his shift and heading to Beaches and Cream to attempt the Kitchen Sink. I'm not proud to say that I wasn't a lot of help; I managed a few scoops of ice cream, and totally took out any and all cherries in the bowl, but it was Cassandra who did the most damage. I watched with respect and envy as the Sink emptied, though we didn't actually finish the entire thing. One more person in our group, though, and we would have conquered it.

Manual's birthday came around, and we made a day of it. YanYing and I came to Chris and Manual's apartment the morning of his birthday and watched him open his presents before we drove to EPCOT. We chatted as we walked to Les Chefs de France, where we had lunch reservations. Waiting for our food, the boys noticed a little kid drawing on a kid's menu. The next thing YanYing and I knew, they had pulled construction paper and crayons (we had brought them to make birthday cards for Manual) out of a bag and were drawing New Zealand (their homeland), discussing weather patterns — the grown-up version of coloring, I suppose. YanYing and I stared at each other, neither of us quite knowing what to do. We rolled our eyes and left them to it, discussing work and the fast-approaching end of our program.

After a phenomenal lunch, we visited a couple of pavilions before YanYing decided she really wanted to go to Image and have our photos taken flying around the Castle. We weren't sure if Manual and Chris would agree, but ten minutes later we were chatting with our friends who were working there, filling out photo vouchers, and leaning up against the wall to watch each other clamber onto the green block and pretend to fly.

Our pictures taken, edited, and printed out, it was time to part ways, and I walked up to the North to change for another shift at package pickup.

December was extremely busy. One of the cooler things that came out of it was the Cast information event held to give the rationale behind the inclusion of James Cameron's *Avatar* in Animal Kingdom. It consisted mostly of a screening of *Avatar* in one of the theatres in Hollywood Studios, but it was quite a cool event. We made our way backstage, past the office where last year I had been dragged in to explain why I had given a woman her shift rotation, and were handed 3D glasses upon entering the theatre. A man tried to explain how the themes involved in *Avatar* echoed those of Animal Kingdom, and how the mythical world of *Avatar* helped to finally incorporate the dragon that was part of the Animal Kingdom signage. It felt like a bit of a stretch to me, but I wasn't complaining about seeing *Avatar* once more in a theatre.

After the movie, YanYing and Manual walked ahead of Chris and me, and as the distance between us increased, Chris and I slowed down to consider the option of going to watch the Osborne Lights again. Chris had become slightly taken with them, and I enjoyed listening to the music and watching the fake snow float down onto the heads of the small children who were totally astonished by everything happening around them. When YanYing and Manual didn't even pause to check if we were behind them as they exited the park, we turned around and made our way back to the Streets of America.

I wanted to participate in Disney's VoluntEARs during my first program, but any time I had had a Sunday or Wednesday free, VoluntEARs had already filled up. At the first Housing meeting, they had passed out information about volunteering to help needy children in a myriad of ways. I worked so much I wasn't able to pin down a time when I could call and they would still have spots open, so when an opportunity finally came up, I jumped at it.

In December, all the locations set up cardboard boxes to collect donations for Toys for Tots. Sign-up sheets were taped to the desks near CDS, and Cassandra signed us both up to help sort toys for the drive.

We awoke early in the morning, and she picked me up at my apartment (the BMW had also stopped working by this point; it was not my fault — something about the alternator messing up). We found our way to a random warehouse that had formerly been some kind of grocery store. We got there early, clad in our Disney VoluntEARs shirts, and signed in. They had bottles of water set out for us, and soon, some men came in and explained how the sorting would work, and we made our way to where all of the donations were stored.

The aisles were labeled, first by age group, then by sex. We were given boxes of trash bags and grocery carts to fill with books, modeling clay, and puzzles that were stored in the freezer sections. Cassandra and I found an aisle that looked like it had the least amount of filled trash bags, and went to work.

It was an absolute blast. There were a certain number of toys and books we were supposed to put in each trash bag, and we had fun making themed bags and matching toys. We quickly found that some dollar store or another had donated hundreds of small army figures, and waged war on them, throwing one into almost every bag we prepared. A system developed, involving some other people who were working in our aisle. Cassandra and I took turns, one picking the two toys that went in the bag, the other adding something from the carts and piling the finished bag into the center of the aisle.

We worked for several hours, and then took a lunch break. The Toys for Tots people had ordered pizzas for all the workers, and we grabbed a few slices and snatched a drink from one of the coolers. We chatted a bit with other Cast Members who had come to volunteer, then it was back to sorting toys. Cassandra and I eventually switched it up and went to put bags together for little girls, where we found toys from our own childhood — and some that were extremely bizarre. As Cassandra loved the princesses, a lot of her bags revolved around them, and I tried to find some of the more less-pink things to put together. All too soon, though, Cassandra and I had to leave; Cassandra had work. We agreed to check our schedules to see if there were more days during which we could volunteer. Sadly, there weren't.

Back at Chatham the next morning, I walked over to Chris' apartment and collapsed in an arm chair, exhausted. Soon, though, we got up and went over to the area near the swimming pool, where the graduation party was being held. We picked up some of the free stuff they were giving out: more posters, a random wind chime, a photo box. Walking around the tables with plates of food in hand, we found Ryan, a friend from Future World, and sat with him, talking about how the end of our program was rapidly approaching. I was feeling sick again, so I wasn't exactly invested in the conversation, and it wasn't long before I was back on a couch, asleep.

At Future World West, the managers arranged a Secret Santa. I got Zhi, an adorable girl from Singapore, and Chris got Amy, one of the part-timers who usually worked the early stock shifts. I'm horrible at these kinds of things; I never know what to get someone, unless I know them particularly well. And as much as Zhi and I said hi to each other and chatted at work, she came to the West after I had been moved to package pickup, which meant that I didn't work with her as often as I did some of the other people there. I ended up buying her a couple of fun things at EPCOT that I would have enjoyed, and I figured would at least serve a basic function, like some of the awesome soaps and lotion from the France Pavilion.

Chris asked me for advice about what to get Amy. I had just chatted with Amy not too long ago, and knew that things had gotten pretty stressful for her. I told him some chocolate, maybe stop by Basin and pick up something, and she would love it. Over at his apartment one night after work, he told me he had gotten Amy's present that day at the outlet mall with Manual. He wouldn't tell me what it was for a moment, and then confessed that he'd been suckered into buying an ice scraper. With a fuzzy handle. For a woman who lived in Florida. I thought for a minute he was joking, but then I realized that this was one of those things you can't make up — it's just too strange.

On the day of the Christmas party at Image, Chris and I made our way to EPCOT, bearing our wrapped presents. We had been promised food and fun; when we got to Image and went upstairs, we found it empty, with a small box holding presents and a table sparsely laid out with an odd assortment of mostly desserts. Richard, Nadine, Britta, and a few others made a brief appearance, but after a while, with still nothing going on, Chris and I left for the Polynesian, where we watched the holiday fireworks from the empty beach — much better than the masses of people I was sure were watching it from Magic Kingdom at that moment.

Of course, my family had come down for Christmas, and I spent Christmas Eve with them at Wilderness Lodge. We woke up relatively early and opened the presents that we had piled up under a tiny tree on the table. My shiny pink wrapping paper was a big hit, as were the stuffed animals that I got as part of the presents for my parents. Later, we went downstairs and had breakfast, sitting out by the pool and enjoying the strangely warm weather on Christmas morning.

I had to go to work, though, and that night I went to Chris and Manual's apartment to exchange Christmas presents with them and YanYing.

Chapter Forty-One

Amber Nears the End

THERE WAS NO HYSTERICAL crying at work. No late night parties with co-workers, no adopted uncles to say goodbye to. As the end of my time with Disney approached, I felt most acutely the difference between my two programs. Yes, during my CareerStart Program there had been a period when I was ready for the program to end. But when the time had come to say goodbye, I wasn't anywhere close to prepared.

As the College Program quickly entered a single-digit countdown, I realized that while I was sad to leave, it was nothing compared to the year before. Chris and Manual were going to South Korea to teach English; Cassandra was staying in Florida for a while to do a professional internship. Richard and Greg were also staying in Florida, so I could return at any point for my *Guitar Hero* re-match with Richard. I had seen my old manager Eddie around EPCOT sometimes on my runs, where he'd promised to get TJ, Stevenson, and I together for something, but nothing ever happened after our dinner together when I'd first arrived. Court was going back to Colorado; Courtney to Kentucky. Ashley, who I desperately wished I'd worked with more, because she was one of the most awesome people I met on the program, was going back to California.

One of the last days on my College Program was New Years. I worked the late shift at package pickup with Cassandra, Jean, Chris, and most of the other package pickup Cast Members. It was a fun day, though a little sad, because it was my last shift. The packages weren't crazy, certainly not as crazy as some of the stories the full-timers told us of days long past, back when package pickup was still in its old location.

Of course, it would be New Years Eve that one of the expensive packages was lost. Someone had bought perfume from the shop in France, and when I had first done that run, the French man that I asked to help me find the package decided he would rather flirt. Finally, I lost my patience, and left without the package, assuming it would turn up later. It didn't, though, and when the guest came looking for it, we called over. It was right before the fireworks were due to go off, and the Chris who worked in package pickup (there were a lot of Christophers on this program) warned me that the roads would be closed, and I would have to walk to the France Pavilion.

Why I didn't turn around when I realized the roads weren't closed, I'm not sure. I kept thinking that maybe later down the road, it would be closed; maybe once I passed under the bridge, they would have blocked off the roads. But they hadn't. And it was a long walk.

Eventually, I made it behind the International Gateway, where I watched in amusement as the fireworks caused most of the car alarms to go off simultaneously. I ventured onstage, slipping in between guests heading toward the exit of the park as I made my way to France.

Lo and behold, behind the counter of the perfume shop, I found not only the package that I had been looking for earlier, but one or two other packages as well. Exasperated, I walked to the backstage area of France and paged base. Jean answered, and I asked him to come pick me up, since it had taken almost twenty minutes just to get to France in the first place.

"What, you mean you walked all the way there?!" he asked incredulously.

"Yeah, well, I was told the roads were closed. By the time I realized they weren't, I was already over halfway here."

Jean kindly got into a van and drove to pick me up. I gave the disgruntled guests their packages, and settled into one of the chairs to pass the rest of the night chatting with Cassandra, waving off Chris' persistent apologies. He had thought the roads would be closed; it was totally fine. It had been a pretty night, and I didn't mind walking that much. Bloody French.

We had a College Program get-together at CiCi's pizza across from Vista Way on one of the last days. Ashley and I talked about music and our mutual love of Doctor Who. Later, I went into work, saying goodbye to people as we shared our last shift together.

Then it was over.

The last night, Cassandra had come over to Chris' apartment, where we had all sat around together and talked. At one point, I fell asleep, and Cassandra was close to sleep herself, stretched out on the couch. She left, though, waking me up to say goodbye. When I woke up the next morning, my father had texted that he was on his way to load everything up and go. Chris and I walked over to my apartment to finish packing (I had already packed most of my stuff, though I never did find my copy of *Peter Pan*, and I had to fish some of my dishes — still dirty — out of the dishwasher). I took out one last load of trash, said goodbye to Chris, and got into the car with Dad.

And we drove away.

It was a strange experience. There wasn't such a feeling of finality that I had experienced after the CareerStart Program. Cassandra and I were determined to stay in touch; her internship has since ended, and she's back in Arizona. We're still planning on visiting soon. Ashley and I stay in touch through Facebook quite often, our love of British television, food, and music making it fun to drop by and share a photo or quote. Chris and I Skyped, emailed, and messaged each other frequently, but a few months after we parted ways, we broke up — we had met working at Image together and started dating a few months into the program. We still keep in contact, though; he's loving his program in Korea and has extended his stay there. Manual is off touring Europe right now, first visiting Taiwan, then Sweden.

I've been down to Disney once since my College Program ended. I said hello to everyone I could find: Stevenson in Fountain View, Richard coordinating in the North, Greg and Rachel working at Image. One of the other women I worked with named Ashley happened to be working then, and we talked about our mutual love of *The Hobbit*. I stopped by the Seas, and ran into Brenda in the France Pavilion as she was doing one of her runs. Grace was visiting at the same time, and I met her at Downtown Disney one night. While I was waiting for her outside Ghirardelli's, I saw Pete walk by, but I don't think he even noticed me. Grace was meeting a few of her other friends, as well, and we ended up going back to Vista Way with one of them. Sitting in his apartment, standing out on the balcony...as much as I had thought I was done with Disney, five months later I found myself nostalgically remembering the numerous sleepovers that had happened in this complex, getting ready for the formal in Betty's apartment, road trips, and orange juice.

It's odd. It feels sometimes as if I did things out of order. High school, college, internship — that's usually the order things go in. Instead, I threw that order out the window, and keep flip-flopping between full-time school, work, and more freedom, then full-time student again.

I meet wonderful people, but once I get to know them, we part ways, never sure when we'll see each other again.

Chapter Forty-Two

Amber at Rest

I STILL HAVE MIXED feelings about my programs. A lot of things I wish I had done differently. A lot of things I find myself remembering in a spare moment, and I realize once again just how potent is the Disney drug.

That's not to say I want to work for them again. While I make a point to avoid the word "never", I would say it's highly unlikely that I will return to work in Disney World.

The CareerStart Program was the pinnacle of what I think one of these programs should be: my job was wonderful and challenging enough to keep me from going insane, my days off were filled, and the people I worked and lived with were absolutely phenomenal.

The College Program, while it comes off most of the time as the program that changed my mind about working for Disney, was a wonderful experience, and I feel like I never do it justice when I tell people about it. Most of my regrets are about this program, though I still haven't worked out what most of them mean. The people I met during my second stint at Disney World were just as fantastic as the people I had come to love on my first program.

Returning to Disney as a guest is a bizarre experience. People often ask if working at Disney "ruined the magic", and I think the person asking the question has the wrong kind of magic in mind. Visiting the parks, even while I was working on the programs, still felt the same as it always had. Knowing the little secret passageways, knowing that beneath my feet were people on break or rushing to clock in, knowing the way a kitchen operates — these things actually made me enjoy my jaunts around the parks more. Even some of the dirty little secrets I became privy to while working there didn't change the way I view Disney World.

It's the memories that "ruined the magic" for me, though not in a bad way. Now, instead of enjoying myself in the park, I think: this was where Lindsey and I had waited in line to see Tiana and took pictures with two little kids; this is where Chris, Lauren, Grace, and I watched Wishes one night; this is where Cassandra and I flew with Peter Pan; and that is the table where I wrote my first published article.

The parks, and the areas around them, are now brimming with fantastic memories, and it's knowing that my life will never again have that kind of stress-free enjoyment, knowing that never again will that group of people be together, caught up in the same kind of energy, that makes me ... not sad, exactly, but wistful. I know the roads leading in and out of Disney World, and still part of me yearns to turn toward Chatham. I still expect to see the gorgeous Sergio serving gelato at the stand outside Italy; I still want to be able to walk into Image and see Ashley, or ring the bell at package pickup and annoy Court.

Those are the kind of memories that make going back to Disney World less enjoyable. As much as I love my family, and our trips to the parks, there's a difference between spending time with your family as you have done for over fifteen years, and going to the parks with new friends, friends that you hope to know for the remainder of your life. Were I to sit in the Fantasmic stadium with my family, I would be looking around to pick out the spots where I sat with Cassandra or Paige. I would watch Captain EO and remember listening to Angel or Steven introducing the show. I would pass Fountain View, and the smell of waffle bowls would not make me hungry, but remind me of the times I stood there and tried not to burn my fingers, or when one of my managers told me his new theory that I was from South Africa.

I would remember standing in Tren-D, debating over my choices for Leah's Easter present, May's bunny and coffee mug safe in hand. "Celebrate You" will play at Magic Kingdom, and I see our unofficial roommate Chris dancing on the couch, Christina, Katie, Katherine, Jordan, Lindsey, and I in hysterics. I remember standing up against the walls of Image chatting with Bo Young or Janelle, standing with

Kim over at the photo wall, taking pictures of Vicky and her family for Christmas. I remember cleaning strollers with Mackenzie and her inviting me to visit her in Washington D.C. I remember working in the North and talking with Hazel, and how she was probably one of the most loved ICPs there. I think of Chatham and remember Katie fighting with Manual in the kitchen of their apartment, and of our last night on the CareerStart Program in Ann's Vacation Club villa. I think of Gemma telling me I have a "small Korean face", and going to Buffalo Wild Wings with Jennifer, Betty, Sarah Mae, and Rachel.

I miss working at Disney on days when my life outside of it gets too stressful. As I worry about buying the required books for all seven of my classes this semester, or as I try to keep myself awake during astronomy lectures, I think back to what I was doing this time a year ago, or two years ago. Inevitably, I was doing something in Florida, having what seems like more fun than I'm having now. As the air starts to cool, I think fondly of walking behind the Seas on one of my runs, driving around the back of EPCOT with the windows down. While, of course, I remember the things that made me to leave the program early, I still catch myself wishing I were back there. Back with the same people, the same feeling of excitement.

I still act like a Cast Member, to an extent. Working in the food industry again, I have to remember that I don't need to clock in five minutes early, or that I am allowed to lean against a counter if it's slow. I have to appear busy if I'm "onstage", a term I still apply to anywhere a customer can see you. I still use the Disney Point (two fingers, never one), and I still have the ability to switch easily into the friendly Cast Member mode at work.

The CareerStart and College Programs. A complicated mess of tears, gelato, late-night video games, and standing in way too many lines. Some people can't wait to leave; I know people — Vicky, Rachel, Briana, Lindsey (who is right now working in Entertainment on Disney's Fantasy cruise ship), among others — who haven't left yet, if they ever will.

I would like to think that I'm done. I can't see a time when I will return to work in the Disney parks; I know what it's like to have high expectations, insurmountable first experiences, and I know that anything that happens after these programs will not measure up.

Twice now, I have put the red "earning my ears" ribbon under my nametag, and I would like to think that by now, I've done it.

About the Author

Amber Sewell lives in Knoxville, Tennessee. Her first visit to Walt Disney World was in 1998; since then, her trips number well over 50. She participated in the Disney CareerStart Program in 2010 and then in the Disney College Program in 2011. She has written articles for DisneyDispatch.com and for *Celebrations* Magazine.

Amber is currently a student at the University of Tennessee, and will graduate with a degree in Creative Writing in 2013.

About the Publisher

Bob McLain founded Theme Park Press in November 2012 to provide well-written, well-edited, world-class print and digital books about Disney theme parks, Disney history, and Disney popular culture.

Our books are available through Amazon, Barnes & Noble, Apple iTunes, Kobo, and at select locations such as the Walt Disney Family Museum. We add new titles frequently.

Our other books include:

- *Who's Afraid of the Song of the South?* - Jim Korkis
- *The Vault of Walt: Volume 1* - Jim Korkis
- *Disneylanders* - Kate Abbott

If you'd like to discuss Theme Park Press publishing *your* book, or helping you get to the point where you have a book to publish, let's talk. We offer generous royalties, vigorous promotion, and author-friendly terms.

To learn more about our books and our authors, please visit:

www.ThemeParkPress.com